THIS IS THE DAY

Readings & meditations
from the Iona Community

Neil Paynter (ed)

WILD GOOSE PUBLICATIONS
www.ionabooks.com

THIS IS THE DAY

CONTENTS

A mouse can do little but a nest of mice can work great havoc.

George MacLeod (Founder of the Iona Community)

INTRODUCTION

Each day of the month Iona Community members pray for one another, for the wider work of the Church, and for their shared concerns. This book explores some of those concerns. These readings and meditations were collected throughout the four years I lived on the Isle of Iona – working as a member of the Iona Community's Resident Group – where I was in very happy charge of buying and selling books, publications and music for the Iona Community's Shop.

It was always exciting when a new book arrived in the shop, tugging open a box to find a new collection by Kathy Galloway or Peter Millar, or from the Wild Goose Resource Group. It was even more exciting to read through the books and to recommend them to people.

Some of the readings in this book are from titles we sold in the shop, while others are taken from the Iona Community's bi-monthly magazine *Coracle* or from previously unpublished works. I have included some favourite readings and some readings used on Iona during the time I was there (for instance, 'I never wanted to be born' and 'God and man and woman', which were often read out on the weekly pilgrimage). There are also some pieces which were written on Iona, and readings which seem, to me, to be 'canon' of the Iona Community.

Also included are short prayers for each day, and a list of scripture readings which readers might like to work through as part of a daily discipline.

The Iona Community believe 'that social and political action leading to justice for all people, and encouraged by prayer and discussion, is a vital work of the church at all levels' (from the Rule of the Iona Community).

I hope that these readings and meditations will aid in prayer and reflection, and serve to encourage thoughtful, committed action in God's world.

This Is the Day was edited on windy, late nights in Cul Dunsmeorach, Iona (once George MacLeod's garage) and, later, in a flat on the mainland. The collection is dedicated to all who believe in the power of the Word (and of words), and to all those who are working to make their communities more just and peaceful places.

I would like to thank everyone who contributed to this book. I wish I could have included more voices but space did not allow it. Thank you also to everyone at Wild Goose Publications for their help and support.

LEADER: THIS IS THE DAY THAT GOD HAS MADE;
ALL: WE WILL REJOICE AND BE GLAD IN IT.
             (from the 'Morning Office' of The Iona Community)

Neil Paynter

'NEW WAYS TO TOUCH THE HEARTS OF ALL'

With imagination and a sense of adventure

I think it is at least arguable that we now live in a post-Christian society and it is indisputable that institutional religion is in decline. I believe that there is a real danger of loss of nerve on the part of the churches. There is a great challenge and opportunity for discovering and experimenting with what the Iona Community describes as 'new ways to touch the hearts of all'. A church-centred approach to mission is unlikely to usher in the kingdom or produce much more than temporary alleviation of present problems. But an approach that reaches out with imagination and a sense of adventure, seeking to reveal where God is already at work in the world, focusing on Jesus Christ and the promise of the kingdom, will lead on to the excitement and surprises that are inevitably part of the way of the spirit.

We must take account of the fact that, however formal religion may have declined, interest in religious and spiritual questions is as strong as ever, and many people still look to the church for leadership. This means that commitment to pursuing social justice through prophecy and service is an essential part of mission, especially in our secular society.

Norman Shanks

ECONOMIC WITNESS

Something must be done about the money boys
Sowing the seeds of the next war?

Fifty years ago, George MacLeod, founder of the Iona Community, wrote these words:

Something must be done about the money boys who run our world. It is urgent that the whole issue of international monetary finance be reviewed.

Have you ever queried the bankers? I have. Try the lower echelon of bankers, and most of them will say, 'These things are too high for us, we cannot attain unto them.' But a small minority will whisper, 'You've got something there, boy; isn't it extraordinarily cold weather for so late in the month of May?'

Try the upper echelon of bankers. I have. I wrote to the top man of a London bank, a charming man, asking his comments on a similar document to the Haslemere Declaration [*a declaration about world poverty*]. He replied that the figures were inaccurate. I immediately asked which figures, but had no reply.

They are in training for the job of international bankers. They know what is good for us. Don't consult us, the paltry crowd. But do they know what is good for us? Or are they sowing the seeds of the next war?

George MacLeod

Prayer

May it not be long, Lord.

May it not be long
   before there are no more beggars at the door
   waiting for the crumbs from the tables of the rich.

May it not be long
   before the northern exploitation
   of the southern economies
   is a fact of history,
   not a fact of life.

May it not be long
   before poor economies
   cease to be havens for sex tourism,
   child labour and experimental genetic farming.

May it not be long
   before those nations we once evangelised
   show us the larger Christ
   whom we, too often, have forgotten.

May it not be long Lord.

May it not be long
   before the governments of our nations
   legislate against commercial avarice
   and over-consumption which hurts the poor
   and indebts them.

Month 1 Day 2

May it not be long
  before Christians in this land
  examine their economic priorities
  in the light of the Gospel,
  rather than in its shadow.

May it not be long
  before we respond out of love,
  not out of guilt.

May it not be long
  before we find wells of hope
  deeper than the shallow pools of optimism
  in which we sometimes paddle.

May it not be long
  before we feel as liberated and addressed
  by your word
  as those first folk did
  who heard you summon the oddest of people
  to fulfil the oddest of callings.

May it not be long, Lord.

Amen

John L. Bell

YOUTH CONCERN

Timothy and Paul

A   Timothy …

B   Yes Paul?

A   I've got a job for you.

B   Uh-uh!

A   Is that any way to speak to an apostle?
Or reply to an epistle, come to that?

B   Right. 'Here am I, send me!'

A   That's better. I'm glad you've read Isaiah.

B   So what is this job?

A   I want you to stay in Ephesus.

B   Oh no, they're weird – they do nothing but talk, arguing over the meaning of
words. Or telling ghost stories.

A   I want you to lead them, gently but firmly, into better ways.

B   Lead them! You wouldn't believe the arguments they have about leadership:
about bishops and deacons and what they should be allowed to do,
and how many wives they should have …
and women – what they can and can't do in church.

A   They need a clear line. I've got some thoughts, and I'll put them down when
I've a minute … But meanwhile I want you to stay there to help them.

B   They won't listen to me. I'm too young.

A   You know what I wrote to the people in Corinth: 'If Timothy comes, see that he
has nothing to fear among you, for he is doing the work of the Lord just as I
am; therefore let no one despise him.'

B Yes Paul, that's fine, but when you're young, people in the churches have a funny way of treating you. They're so keen for you to be there: 'Look, we've got a real live young person!' But they don't know what to do with you … how to listen to what you're really saying … your story … or how to use your gifts.

A Don't let anyone despise your youth.

B That's easy for you to say!

A Just be yourself. Recognise that God's made you a special person – with a vision, with words to share it; a person who really cares for other people. *Do not neglect the gift that is in you.*

B Oh Paul!

A Oh yes, Timothy!

Jan Sutch Pickard

THE WORD

What's special about the Bible?

She was a shy African woman. When teased by her loud-mouthed neighbour, she was tongue-tied, unable to produce a ready answer to her taunts. The reason for the scorn which was heaped upon her was the place that the shy woman gave to the Bible. Not only did she read it regularly; if any problem or dilemma faced her which she found difficult to cope with, she would go into her hut, turn to passages which she thought might help her, meditate upon them, then emerge to deal with the situation.

Things came to a head. In front of others, the neighbour took her to task. 'There are all kinds of books in the world which can help us find how to live,' she said, 'yet you turn to just one, always the same one. Why, tell me, why? Why this one book?'

At last, the woman's tongue was loosed, the words came. 'Other books I read,' she said. 'This book reads me.'

Ian M Fraser

Hospitality and Welcome

The guests were starting to arrive for the centenary celebration, and the deaconess was standing at the door waiting to greet the new mayor. She wondered how she would recognise him, but was assured that other people wouldn't be wearing chains around their necks.

When a chauffeur-driven car pulled up at the specially cordoned-off area, she came forward and greeted the impressive-looking gentleman who emerged, and led him into the building. But after being introduced to one or two people, he tactfully informed her that he was not the new mayor! She apologised profusely, only grateful that she had not already ushered him to a VIP seat.

Meanwhile, however, she had missed the real mayor. He had passed her in the corridor, but how could she have known? Not only was he chainless; he looked so ordinary! Furthermore, he had walked to the church, and come in at the back door. It was the caretaker who pointed him out to her. 'Yes, I know Bert,' he said. 'I used to do the soup run with him.'

Jesus, are you the one?
It is hardly surprising that people missed your coming
when even John the Baptist wasn't sure.

They were expecting such a different kind of messiah.
The unmistakable kind.
Chauffeur-driven, on a VIP throne, with a gold chain.
How could anyone be expected to know who you were
when you came in the back, looking ordinary?

There were plenty who did recognise you, of course:
the blind man who cried, 'Son of David, have pity!',
the disturbed one who screamed, 'Stay away!',
the woman who touched the hem of your coat,
the folk who knew you from the soup run.
But are you the one, Jesus? We still have to ask.
In a world of paths and promises, how can we be sure?
Your reply is your work amongst the sick and oppressed.
'Decide for yourselves!' you say –
as if it isn't the doctrines, or even the miracles,
but the company you keep and the priorities you hold,
and the kingdom of possibilities and joy
you unpack amid our ordinariness.

So help us to be on the look-out for your coming,
as people and events crowd in.
Open our eyes to see you in the guise of friend and stranger.
Whatever the path, wherever the place,
however you come to us,
may there be recognition.
And joyous welcoming.

Brian Woodcock

THIS IS THE DAY

The reawakening to mystery is leading us to an attentiveness to the present moment. One of the psalms that I love expresses that so powerfully when it says: 'This is the day that the Lord has made. Let us rejoice and be glad in it.' The possibility and preciousness of the moment. This moment that we're given is, in itself, a precious moment and we ourselves are precious within it.

One of the hallmarks of contemporary society is that we tend to live in the future. But this psalm reminds us, as do many passages in scripture, that we are not future tense people but we live in the moment of possibility now. The possibility that is inherent in the present moment. 'Life,' as one commentator said, 'is not a dress rehearsal. It is now.' This is the moment of pilgrimage, of possibility, of truth.

Peter Millar

Leader	This is the day that God has made;
ALL:	WE WILL REJOICE AND BE GLAD IN IT.
Leader:	We will not offer to God
ALL:	OFFERINGS THAT COST US NOTHING.
Leader:	Go in peace to love and to serve;
ALL:	WE WILL SEEK PEACE AND PURSUE IT.
Leader:	In the name of the Trinity of Love,
ALL:	GOD IN COMMUNITY, HOLY AND ONE.

from the Morning Service (*Iona Abbey Worship Book*)

Month 1 Day 6

THE IONA EXPERIENCE

Why Iona?

God is present everywhere, and can be sought and encountered even, and perhaps especially vividly, in places of greatest need. But there are also some places which in their clarity and peace render people particularly open to experience God, where the veil that separates the earth and the Kingdom seems tissue-thin. Iona has been such a place for countless generations of pilgrims.

(from *What is The Iona Community?*)

Iona dance

Somehow the air seems to dance differently here,
executing a perfect back-flip into the arms of the short-cropped hillsides,
gliding in sequinned splendour and perfect three-four time
across the machair,
juggling with rooks and tossing them ragged,
into the raw wind,
swaying, arms entwined, with the green flags
and the surprised white daisies,
somersaulting spectacularly over the cotton grass,
jitterbugging with the spray and
jiving with the spinning sun-specks
over the water,
tapping in time with the tip-tapping pebbles
as they partner the dinner-jacketed oyster-catchers,
line dancing on the telephone wires
to the hum of other people's messages,
smooching in a long, last waltz with the silver sands …
somehow, here, the air just dances.

Alix Brown

LIFE IN COMMUNITY

Volunteers

Life in community, Iona 1938
'To accept each other essentially'

We were all volunteers. All of us had left our normal occupations to join the Community. Whatever our religious, social or political beliefs and practices, by joining the Community we were ultimately responding to a desire, or need, within ourselves, to work at something which gives us in return something more, something other and different, than bread alone. We were volunteers to that fundamental impulse within us, which we wanted to find expression in the realisation of the ideal on which the Iona Community rested. That the impulse was, for the most part, unconscious, does not mean that it was less powerful; quite the contrary. Nor was it entirely unconscious. That we were all dressed alike, ate the same food, lived under identical conditions and so on, was but a symbolic recognition of our common spirit; and expression of our readiness to value (a man) not by any other standard than the quality and force of that spirit (in him). Having that essential superficial difference; we found scope in the Community for our profound and mighty similarity, which from the first was a bond between us and made us accept each other essentially. It was not, therefore, so very remarkable that, in spite of our individualities and apparent dissimilarities, we quickly became a true community. This became manifest not only in our family prayers, in our work and recreation, but also in the communal nature of our disagreements.

A volunteer, 1938

Volunteers

Life in community, Iona 2000
Sharing our stories

… Alice (who used to sell antique jewellery talking about a bonfire on the beach: how she stood and watched the waves steam and hiss; how she can see things here, *really* see things. How the other day the sea was like silver. And the crest of a wave – the very top that hung there – like a peridot she sold one time. How she's seeing things have a different value now. A new preciousness.

Julie sharing how one morning she ran up Dun I chasing after the sunrise – explaining she has migraines usually that keep her down. But that one clear morning she woke up early and looked out, and ran up Dun I. Climbed thinking about how she could never find her niche in life, was always chasing after something, never catching up. And needed to reach the top before the sunrise, and arms outstretched made it, and cried and laughed. Then thought about all the prisoners in the world who never even see the sun. Then, how we are all prisoners in ourselves. And prayed for all prisoners.

Lynne, beautiful Lynne talking about playing her recorder in a communion service. And how in the perfect silence after the last whole note she felt someone else there besides her. *Beside her*. About how God speaks in silences.

Moments listening to friends. The feeling in the moment after of something holy that hangs in the air. The resonance of something beyond words. Like the feeling you experience after listening to a beautiful poem, or song, or prayer. In the moment after the breaking of the bread with the wine held up.

Com-panion.

Moments in meetings:
The cook who shared how she had lost her taste for life, and found its savour again here – can taste, smell, feel again. Thank you, Lord. How, in the end, she told us, it was she who was fed.

Month 1 Day 8

Someone else saying they feel at home: at home in themselves. And that they are learning to feel the grace through the sorrow. 'The deeper joy within.'

The warm smell of the kitchen reaching in as we share our stories: This life like the rich, healthy smell of crusty brown bread with wholemeal flour, malt, honey, caraway seeds …

***

Moments talking to guests: after service; at tea time: about where they've come from, where they're going.

A guest from the inner city who came to get away from the drink and drugs, and just breathe in the peace and quiet.

An eighty-year-old woman from Hertfordshire who found a plastic bucket and spade down on the north beach, and spent the whole day making a sand sculpture out of stones and shells. 'It must have been left there for some reason,' she said and smiled, her life-lined face lit up. Like a little girl's again.

A gentleman from America whom I met in the abbey library, and got talking to about journeys. (Outside a wintery wind cried and knocked. The library felt intimate and warm. Filled with God's enfolding presence.)

We sat down together, and he explained that he had cancer; that he was dying – but wasn't afraid any longer. Once you finally accept it, he said, you get all you can out of life. Every moment is precious. 'You want to tell everybody you meet that,' he said, and looked at me. He was concerned for his friends though, they were all still afraid, and as he quietly, gently spoke I could feel myself opening up to precious life again.

'So, what are you reading?' he asked and smiled.

Do not be afraid, in his eyes.

A retired businessman who came to work and worship.
A busy nurse who came to be still.
Volunteers from Uganda, Pakistan, Norway, Germany, the Sudan …
A priest who works with refugees on the Texas/Mexico border.
A group from L'Arche.
Teens from Birmingham.

Month 1 Day 8

Someone who came alone to see.

The moment when all these different people – men and women, young and old, rich and poor – begin to understand each other; come together like members of a choir, and the whole Centre sings with an energy. Rushes with a spirit …

Neil Paynter

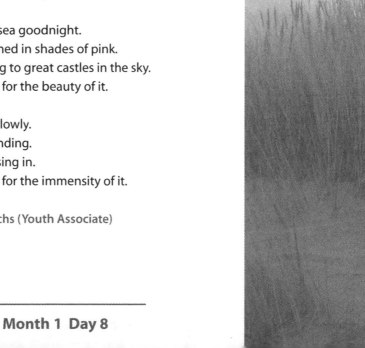

Top of Dun I

Wind blowing in my face.
Clinging to the rocks.
At the mercy of nature's forces.
I can't breathe – for the power of it.

Sun kissing the sea goodnight.
Distant hills bathed in shades of pink.
Clouds gathering to great castles in the sky.
I can't breathe – for the beauty of it.

Colours fading slowly.
Darkness descending.
Deep peace closing in.
I can't breathe – for the immensity of it.

Jenni Sophia Fuchs (Youth Associate)

WOMEN

God and man and woman

This can be read by two people standing apart, allowing for pauses for thought and laughter as appropriate.

A: In the beginning, God made man.
     He was so disappointed that he tried again,

     and the next time, he made woman.

B: Eve, the first woman, was a vegetarian.
     She liked apples, and ate the wrong one.

     Men have been suspicious of vegetarians ever since.

A: Noah didn't eat apples.
     He was a man … so he drank alcohol.
     In fact, he drank so much alcohol that one day
     his sons found their old man completely sozzled
     and lying in the nude.

     Women have been suspicious of alcohol ever since.

B: Lot didn't eat apples or drink wine.
     He just lived in a city where the men didn't know who they fancied.
     So God told him to leave the city, and so he did.

God said, 'Don't look back, for I'm going to burn down the city.'
So Lot didn't look back, but his wife did
and she turned into a pillar of salt.

Women have never looked back since.

A: Delilah didn't eat apples, drink wine or look back.
She was a hairdresser.
Samson didn't know that,
but while he was resting his macho muscles,
Delilah cut his hair and took his strength away.

Men have avoided being bald ever since.

B: St Paul didn't know Eve, Noah, Lot or Delilah.
But he did know some women,
and those he did must have given him bad memories.
Because he told them not to speak in church,
not to go into church without a hat
and always to obey their husbands.
Paul also said that men shouldn't get married
unless they were unable to control themselves.

Men have been unable to control themselves ever since.

A: But Jesus was different.

He was strong, but he cried.
He even cried in front of other men.
He knew that some women had bad reputations,
but that didn't keep him back from them:
he knelt beside them.

Month 1 Day 9

He loved his disciples who were all men
and he wasn't afraid to tell them that he loved them.
And though he was never married,
he was always surrounded by women who, at his death,
were more faithful to him than the men.

Jesus didn't make a fuss about who was who, or who was what.
He said that everyone who loved him was his mother

his sister
his brother.

A&B: Thank God for Jesus.

John L. Bell & Graham Maule

Month 1 Day 9

PRAYER

Give us this day our daily bread
Bread for everyone

There are many ceremonies in our culture around meals, and Jesus constantly used feasts, meals and the table where all were welcome as a sign of the Kingdom. We ignore the ceremony of meals at our cost. And how many of us maintain the ceremony of giving thanks for food? Perhaps it is too uncomfortable for us, when we know that others starve while we eat. All the more reason to give thanks, and to remember that to pray 'Give us this day our daily bread' is a prayer of anguish for millions.

Kathy Galloway

Grace

Making bread –
squishy dough
moist feel
smelling of yeast,
punching, kneading
folding in air –
hard working hands.

White, brown, granary,
soft or crusty –
now we're baking!
Hot –
hungry smell.

Breaking, eating, sharing
Bread for everyone –
Communion!

Daniel Rounds, Samantha Jones & Greg Jones
(three children staying at the MacLeod Centre)

JUSTICE AND PEACE

Not an optional extra
Transformed at a profound personal level

The late Archbishop Oscar Romero of El Salvador, who was assassinated because of his commitment to the marginalised, once wrote: 'I am a shepherd who, with his people, has begun to learn the beautiful and difficult truth: our Christian faith requires that we submerge ourselves in this world.'

The Iona Community's roots are in Govan in Glasgow, where poverty and unemployment have been markers of the common life. The Community believes that the Gospel commands us to seek peace founded on lasting justice and that only costly reconciliation is at the heart of the Christian message. At the end of an extraordinarily violent century, it continues to believe that, both locally and globally, work for justice, peace, an equitable society and the care of creation are matters of extreme urgency for the churches around the world.

Today, as we listen to the cries of the voiceless, the marginalised, the impoverished, the abused, the exploited and the tortured, we hear clearly the cries of Christ, the One who took on himself the sufferings and injustices of the world. And continues to do so.

This commitment to justice and peace is not an 'optional extra' for Christians. Rather, it is an imperative of the Gospel, and perhaps especially in our time when many of our global structures are permeated with almost unimaginable injustices. The theologian Ronald Sider once expressed this commitment succinctly when he wrote: 'Christian churches should not be comfortable clubs of conformity but communities of loving defiance.'

Our prayers and reflections concerning these great issues are points of departure, propelling us to action. And in that movement of solidarity we ourselves are transformed at a profound spiritual level. Some words written by Joyce Gunn Cairns, a member of the Iona Community, are both inspiring and challenging as we seek to hold God's world in our prayers. Joyce wrote: 'The people in prison whom I visit have honoured me with the gift of their vulnerability. Many of them are able to discern the true freedom that comes when one is stripped of all status, and it is thus that they can teach me something about the meaning of spiritual poverty. In coming to serve the poor, so to speak, I am discovering that I am poor.'

Peter Millar

THE INTEGRITY OF CREATION

A new awareness is required

The material is shot through with the spiritual: there is a 'withinness' of God in all life. The whole earth is sacramental: every thing is truly every blessed thing, and it is indeed blasphemy to use the very atom to kill.

In this life of God, who is both cosmic Lord and personal lover, we see how the personal and the corporate are indissolubly linked. Reverence for the earth, God's sacrament, is not only right and fitting, it is essential for the survival of the planet. So it is too with reverence for people, bearers also of the life of God. The image of man as dominant exploiter of the earth must be replaced by that of man as steward of God's creation, holding all things in trust.

For things which are 'second nature' to be displaced, a new awareness is required. Reverence for people and reverence for the earth are not new, but they are certainly radical.

Ron Ferguson

Prayer

Invisible we see you, Christ beneath us.
With earthly eyes we see beneath us stones and dust
and dross, fit subjects for the analyst's table.
But with the eye of faith, we know you uphold.
In you all things consist and hang together:
the very atom is light energy,
the grass is vibrant,
the rocks pulsate.

All is in flux; turn but a stone and an angel moves.

George MacLeod

COLUMBAN CHRISTIANITY & THE CELTIC TRADITION

A balanced rhythm

The early Irish monks ... understood the basic rhythm of Christian life and the need to balance activity in the world and withdrawal from it. The ideal of *peregrinatio* involved a certain degree of exile, renunciation and searching for one's own desert place of resurrection. Except for those few called permanently to the solitary eremitical life of the anchorite, however, it did not mean a complete withdrawal from the world and its affairs. The monastic life was far from being one of retreat and escape. Indeed, monasteries were almost certainly the busiest institutions in Celtic society, constantly teeming with people and fulfilling the roles of school, library, hospital, guest house, arts centre and mission station. Most of the great Celtic saints alternated between periods of intense activity and involvement in administrative affairs with lengthy spells of quiet reflection and months spent alone in a cell on a remote island or rocky promontory. In this, they were following the example of their Lord and Saviour, one moment surrounded by crowds and engaged in preaching, teaching and healing, and the next walking alone by the lakeside or engaged in quiet prayer in the mountains.

Columba's life exemplified this balanced rhythm. At times he was busily engaged in founding monasteries, negotiating with kings, attending councils, going on missionary journeys and ruling his ever-expanding monastic *familia*. Yet his biographers also portray him spending long periods praying or copying Scriptures in his cell and he frequently took himself to Hinba for solitary retreats. In many ways this combination of action and meditation provided a perfect example of what modern theologians call 'praxis' – a combination of involvement in practical issues and theological reflection on them. In the words of a poem written about him just a year or two after his death, 'What he conceived keeping vigil, by action he ascertained.'[1]

Ian Bradley

RACISM

The lure of monoculture

The people who built the Tower of Babel had only one language, and their sole purpose was to prove to themselves and to anyone else watching how superior they were. They did this by trying to demonstrate that big was best, building a monument to their own conceit to prove the point. And God would not tolerate it.

When any building, any enterprise, becomes an all-consuming passion, it displaces God and with God all those whom God shelters – the poor, the weak, the marginalised.

In this light, we may see the history of civilisation as a story of rival nations struggling to become global powers and enforcing uniformity on the world. The British did that by colouring pink as much of the map as was possible, requiring English to be the lingua franca, and expecting people who knew nothing of London nevertheless to vow unswerving obedience to a monarch resident in that city.

In the process of building the Empire, Indians were transported to work in Central Africa, and West Coast Africans were transported in shackles and by the millions to become slaves on the eastern seaboard of the New World.

A contemporary example of the same phenomenon may be seen as the World Bank and the International Monetary Fund (both misnomers given that they are controlled by the West!) commend and impose Northern patterns of economic development unsuited to Southern-hemisphere nations. Hence the impoverished nation of Uganda, a former British colony, spends 4 per cent of its income on education, 3 per cent on health and over 14 per cent on paying back interest on loans from the North.

Similar patterns of imposed uniformity can be seen in the boasts of the mighty fast food chains that all over the world billions of their products are eaten every day. The cost to the earth which such proud empires exact, in their requirement that Central American forest lands be denuded of trees in order that beef cattle may safely graze, has yet to be properly calculated.

The Babylonian tower phenomenon was also evident in Scotland in the 60s and 70s when locally owned manufacturing industries were bought up by multinational companies which, before long, transferred production to cheaper parts of the globe and put thousands of workers on the dole. This was certainly the case in my own native town when eight major industries changed hands in almost as many years.

Oh, how I wish that then I hadn't kept the Bible so apart from my life that it did not inform it! Oh, how I wish that then I had seen in this odd story of the Tower of Babel God's adamant opposition to proud empires and enterprises whose primary goal is self-aggrandisement, never mind the cost or casualties in the wake.

We are not destined to be a monoculture, to be uniform. The differences that exist among nations and cultures, that make other people hard to understand or attractive, are there by divine design.

So, if you should happen to end up on the Costa Brava and no waiter can fulfil your need for a fish supper or hot-pea special, then thank God. And if you should end up in Rome and find it odd to be buying a cup of tea with lire rather than pounds sterling, thank God. And if you go into the West End of Glasgow and see second and third generation Pakistani or Indian restaurateurs offering a range of curries which no cholesterol-saturated white Glaswegian could ever make, then thank God for this glorious diversity.

John L. Bell

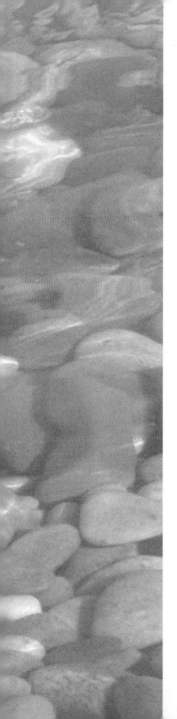

Prayer

Dear God, we thank you for
the richness, gifts and contributions
of different cultures

We thank you for:

Nelson Mandela
Archbishop Desmond Tutu
Aung San Suu Kyi
Mahatma Gandhi

For Ray Charles singing *Georgia* and
Little Richard singing *Tutti Frutti Oh Rudy*

For the vocal harmonies of Ladysmith Black Mambazo

For Boogie Woogie
Be Bop
Jazz
Rap
Funk
Soul
Rock 'n' Roll

Salsa clubs
The samba
Spirituals and voices
deep and profound as wells of living water

For the heady smell of the Indian grocers
For cardamom, saffron, cloves
Jasmine, patchouli, sandalwood

Month 1 Day 14

For the music of accents
dance of gestures
communication of smiles

For the lined landscapes of beautiful faces

For kebabs
hummus
baklava
goulash
won ton soup
warm naan bread
tandoori
sweet and sour
rice and peas and curried goat

For Greek delicatessens
Arabic delicatessens
Italian delicatessens
For delicatessens!

For gold jewellery against black skin
the sound of reggae from the car repair shop
the pungent, sour smell of indigo-dyed cloth
the blast and blare of Notting Hill Carnival

Neil Paynter and others

COMMUNITY

God sets us in community

For we are not trying to build community. We can never do that. God sets us in community and it is man's sin that he is always breaking it. God has set us in inescapable community, in our family, in our neighbourhood, in all the relationships with others that life brings. And all the time we rebel. All the time we kick against the pricks. When we are enlivened by the Spirit of Christ we accept community and begin to live according to the laws of our being.

Ralph Morton, 1951

Pilgrimage

Pilgrimage is traditionally a journey to a holy place – a place where saints have walked, a place where God has met people and blessed them.

People through the ages have journeyed with God on pilgrimage – to perform a penance, to ask for healing, to pray for places where there is war or national disaster, to pray for friends.

Pilgrimage is an opportunity to travel lightly, to walk free of daily routines, to meet people, to make friends, to enjoy and celebrate God's creation. An opportunity too in the travelling, the conversations and the silences to reflect on the journey of our lives and on our journey homewards to God.

Prayers before setting out on a pilgrimage

God of the guiding star, the bush that blazes
SHOW US YOUR WAY
God of the stormy seas, the bread that nourishes
TEACH US YOUR TRUTH
God of the still, small voice, the wind that blows where it chooses
FILL US WITH LIFE
God of the elements, of our inward and outward journeys
SET OUR FEET ON YOUR ROAD TODAY

MAY GOD BLESS US WITH A SAFE JOURNEY
MAY THE ANGELS AND SAINTS TRAVEL WITH US
MAY WE LIVE THIS DAY IN JUSTICE AND JOY
AMEN

Ruth Burgess

SEXUALITY

'It's in the arms of my lover, in the heartstopping vulnerability of that moment when I am loved and accepted for what I am … that I know there is a God who enjoys life.'

Anna Briggs

Divided people

Two thousand years ago, Paul struggled heroically to construct a meaningful framework to explain the existence and persistence of human wrongdoing, and to show how Jesus offered a way beyond its dreary inevitability. And indeed, few have charted the *experience* of sin more profoundly. His way of addressing it, of interpreting its causes, was to split the human person into two parts.

Paul's struggle, owing much as it did to the Greek mind/body dualism of the time, is a profound and insightful description of the feelings, the inner experience, of conflicting desires and values, not least of his own feelings. But that struggle has actually resulted in what he himself describes: 'I don't do the good I want to do; instead I do the evil that I don't want to do.' (*Romans 7:19*)

There can be few doctrines that have been so damaging to so many, can have so defaced the image of God as one which splits the human person into parts and declares the physical intrinsically bad. Still today, lovers and counsellors, therapists and doctors are helping to pick up the pieces of lives blighted by this interpretation. It has allowed all that is sensory and feeling, all that is instinctive and intuitive to be despised, and the intellectual and 'spiritual' to be idolised. It has deprived countless men and women and children of the experience of much of what is most delightful, most hopeful and most joyful about being human. It has divided people against themselves, against each other, and against God.

Kathy Galloway

Month 1 Day 17

HEALING

The undeniable need for absolution

We have a service every Tuesday night in the Abbey on Iona, in which we pray by name for people who are sick, and lay hands on any who wish to receive this ministry. Over many years of participating in this service, I have been forced to ask questions, and draw some conclusions. By far the largest number who come to receive the laying-on of hands are people who fall into a category which might be broadly termed those in search of spiritual healing. But even then, there are many people who come forward who I know are not troubled in their faith, who are not despondent and cast down beyond what is usual, who are not in mourning or addicts or whatever. People go forward to receive the laying-on of hands to be healed of anger, of greed, of fear, of selfishness and of all the other things that make all of us broken people. People in large numbers, perhaps sixty or seventy at a time, and many of them young people, receive the laying-on of hands because they are seeking absolution. And a ceremony in which we invoke the presence of God's spirit, and symbolise our care as a church by our touch, makes that absolution real to people. Touch is such a basic human need, and something that is so often alien to our culture, especially for men, that when it is received in a way that is non-threatening, it comes as a real liberation. It is an experience of grace, a moment of making whole. It is, if you like, a sacrament.

Kathy Galloway

A touching place

(tune: Dream Angus, Scottish traditional)

Christ's is the world in which we move,
Christ's are the folk we're summoned to love,
Christ's is the voice which calls us to care,
and Christ is the one who meets us here.

Chorus: To the lost Christ shows his face;
           to the unloved he gives his embrace;
           to those who cry in pain or disgrace,
           Christ makes, with his friends, a touching place.

Feel for the people we most avoid,
strange or bereaved or never employed;
feel for the women, and feel for the men
who fear that their living is all in vain.

Feel for the parents who've lost their child,
feel for the women whom men have defiled,
feel for the baby for whom there's no breast,
and feel for the weary who find no rest.

Feel for the lives by life confused,
riddled with doubt, in loving abused;
feel for the lonely heart, conscious of sin,
which longs to be pure but fears to begin.

John L. Bell and Graham Maule

SOCIAL ACTION

'The seventh war from now'

I am reminded of the story of a Vietnam protester who sat on the pavement holding a poster. When he was asked what he was trying to do he replied: 'I am trying to stop the seventh war from now.'

Roger Gray

The system

You feel very, very small on an action, and you are afraid, because challenging the system and seeming to break the law are not undertaken lightly. There's always a bit of you scared stiff, so you feel extremely vulnerable and powerless. You are tempted to wonder, 'Isn't this a complete waste of time?' Until the action is over! Then, when you have made your protest, acted out your deepest convictions, you may be rewarded with a wonderful peace of mind. Also the amazing realisation dawns that all the military panoply that you have been opposing was actually scared of you and your friends who challenged them with nothing but their faith, their prayers, and their hopes for the future. I find that a very powerful lesson about being a Christian.

Maire-Colette Wilkie

CHURCH RENEWAL

A counter-cultural vision and an eagerness to celebrate

The Church's vocation in each and every locality is to be a worshipping, healing, learning, serving community, faithfully living by the values of the kingdom, modelling and embodying a counter-cultural vision, looking and reaching out beyond itself with a wider vision, to discover the light and love of God in engagement with the life of the world, standing up and speaking out against all that diminishes and disempowers humanity. In so doing it will dream and explore; it will be open, flexible and ready to take risks; it will be generous, hospitable and ready to celebrate; it will not be a ghetto but keen to co-operate and engage; it will be a transforming community – influencing others for good, and being transformed itself in the process; it will be resilient and persistent, however hard the way, and it will be marked by joy and an eagerness to celebrate.

Norman Shanks

WORSHIP

The wrong tune

The shame of the Church is its attempt to limit authentic worship to one or possibly a few traditions, regarding the worship of other traditions as less than authentic. This tendency leads to exclusivism. 'I liked the words of that hymn,' says a worshipper, 'but why do we sing it to the wrong tune?' If I come into an unfamiliar church service on a holiday Sunday and I see the number of my favourite hymn on the hymnboard, I feel at home immediately … That is, until the organist strikes up what I have the effrontery to call 'the wrong tune'. The 'wrong tune' syndrome is the bugbear of organists and liturgists throughout the Church and it displays the conservative inertia of much Christian worship. A good tune cannot be a wrong tune; it can only be an unfamiliar tune. If such exclusivism were confined to the Church's worship, it would be sad but not serious. What is serious is the determination of many Christians to regard traditions other than their own as handicapped, limited, 'less than the full shilling'. When this determination spills out from Sunday worship into the working world, the dangers multiply. In the West of Scotland, the job interview goes fine until you are asked what school you went to – then the thumbs go down. You want a house in a better part of the city, but the Orange–Green divide is against you. Your children walk a long road to school, because the local school is not for them. We like to think our society, at least east of the Irish Sea, is run on open lines, but ethnic exclusivism is not a Serbian monopoly.

Maxwell Craig

WORK

Genesis 1 & 2: Iona

Today I glimpse chaos:
clouds swirling down the mountains,
waves running before the wind,
gusts battering the walls;
ferries cancelled, plans banjaxed.

Today I glimpse God at work:
moving on the waters,
brooding on the abyss,
breathing life into our clay –
creating new possibilities: seeing the good.

Today I get down to work:
out of chaos imagining God.

Knowing my place in creation,
I begin to name what I see.

Jan Sutch Pickard

CALLED TO BE ONE

In any event

At various times I have attended services at a dozen branches of the Church, from the colour and majesty of the Russian Orthodox liturgy to the lovely simplicity of the Quaker Meeting, and including Roman Catholic and Free Presbyterian, in places as far apart as a monastery in Russia and the top of Arthur's Seat at dawn of a May morning, when streams of pilgrims may be seen converging on the summit, and in all places and at all times I have felt and believed myself to be part of the body with which I was worshipping.

But in any event how trifling and unimportant are the things on which we differ compared with the wonder and glory of the faith we have in common, a faith which, if applied, would lead to the transformation of the whole of humanity in a twinkling of an eye.

Roger Gray

MISSION

Doing mission Jesus's way

'You know, I remember one member of our theology group saying the problem with the church is that it doesn't do mission Jesus's way. Because all the church does, in its mission, is it gives answers. Whereas Jesus normally, by the stories he told, and by the way he did things, presented people with questions. And so she said what we should be doing in terms of mission is doing mission in Jesus's way, which is going and asking people questions. And I see, yes, that's totally true but, in one sense, all these years of training had simply equipped me better and better to provide answers.'

Martin Johnstone

THE POOR AND DISADVANTAGED

Nothing blurred there either!

Do we really believe that the God who called the rulers of Israel to task; who brought the rich women of Jerusalem to heel; who witnessed the worth and dignity of the poor widow, wants us to be silent on these issues and thus free to promote private religiosity?

The prophet Jeremiah says, 'Doomed is the man who builds his house by injustice and enlarges it by dishonesty; who makes his countrymen work for nothing and does not pay their wages. Doomed is the man who says, "I will build myself a mansion with spacious rooms upstairs." So he puts windows in his house, panels it with cedar and paints it red. Does it make you a better king if you build houses of cedar finer than those of others? Your father enjoyed a full life, he was always just and fair and he prospered in everything he did. He gave the poor a fair trial and all went well with him.'

The prophet Isaiah writes, 'God says, "When you lift your hands in prayer, I will not look at you. No matter how much you pray, I will not listen, for your hands are covered with blood. Wash yourselves clean. Stop all this evil that I see you doing. Yes, stop doing evil and learn to do right. See that justice is done – help those who are oppressed, give orphans their rights and defend widows … the city that once was faithful is behaving like a whore … your leaders are rebels and friends of thieves; they are always accepting gifts and bribes. They never defend orphans in court or listen when widows present their case." '

The Lord said, 'Look how proud the women of Jerusalem are! They walk along with their noses in the air. They are always flirting. They take dainty little steps and the bracelets on their ankles jingle. But I will punish them – I will shave their heads and leave them bald.'

A day is coming when the Lord will take away from the women of Jerusalem everything they are so proud of – the ornaments they wear on their ankles, on their heads, on their necks, and on their wrists. He will take away their veils and their hats; the magic charms they wear on their arms and at their waists; the rings they wear on their fingers and in their noses, all their fine robes, gowns, cloaks and purses, their revealing garments, their linen handkerchiefs and the scarves and long veils they wear on their heads. Instead of using perfumes, they will stink; instead of fine belts they will wear coarse robes; instead of having beautiful hair, they will be bald; instead of fine clothes they will be dressed in rags; their beauty will be turned to shame!

It is recorded that, as Jesus sat near the temple treasury, he watched the people as they dropped in their money. Many rich men dropped in a lot of money; then a poor widow came along and dropped in two little copper coins worth about a penny. He called his disciples together and said to them, 'I tell you that this poor widow put more in the offering box than all the others. For the others put in what they had to spare of their riches; but she, poor as she is, put in all she had – she gave all she had to live on.'

The Bible also tells us, 'God chose the poor people of this world to be rich in faith and to possess the kingdom which he promised to those who love him. But you dishonour the poor! Who are the ones who oppress you and drag you before the judges? The rich! They are the ones who speak evil of that good name which has been given to you.'

Nothing blurred there either!

Erik Cramb

INTERFAITH

A God of Justice and Mercy

Dr Salah suddenly asked me one day, 'Do you believe in God?' I replied, 'Yes, I could never have done what I have been able to do if I had not had a firm faith in God, and it is my faith that keeps me going even though things do look bleak.' He said that he, too, had only been able to survive throughout the years of the civil war in Lebanon and to participate in the struggles of his people because he believed in God. He is a Muslim, I am a Christian, we both have our different beliefs and ways of worshipping God, but we both believe in a God of Justice and Mercy.

Prayer

In you, O God of life, I place my hope
my great hope, my living hope, this day and evermore.

Runa Mackay

NONVIOLENCE AND PEACEKEEPING

Testimony – Not possible to sit on the fence

'Moderator: I beg to move the motion in my name calling on Her Majesty's Government now to pursue a policy of nuclear disarmament. It is nineteen years since I first spoke to an Assembly of my belief that opposition to the possession of nuclear weapons is an imperative of the Christian faith, since it is not possible, in practice or theory, to possess them without being prepared to use them. One of the lessons I have learned in twenty-three years' active involvement in the peace movement is that few people are persuaded to change their views – and certainly not in five minutes – by arguments, and so, instead of arguing the cause of unilateralism, I shall follow the example of Christians over the last two thousand years, and give my testimony.

'I am a born-again Christian and, like Billy Graham and many others, I have had two subsequent conversions. As a result, I recently retired from my work as an optician so that I might do more work in the peace movement. One of my first actions was to visit Greenham Common, as I just could not believe the stories I had heard of the determination and power, as well as the enthusiasm and love, of the few women who camped there.

'I walked all the nine miles around the base, saw all the women's camps, and spoke to every member of the forces, American as well as British, that I met.

'I expected to be overwhelmed by a sense of evil in the presence of weapons which could start a process which could lead to the destruction of life on this planet, and would certainly destroy all the values we were trying to defend, but could not feel any sense of evil, no matter how hard I tried. As I had my lunch in the woods in that lovely part of our countryside, sitting on the dry autumn leaves, with the sun shining, I realised that not only all wisdom and morality but all power rested with the few women in the camps outside and the multitudes, of women and men, who are behind them. And I realised not for the first time that, whether we wish it, or even believe it, each one of us is, by our actions, choosing between the darkness of death and the light of life, because there is nothing in between.

'In one sense that is not quite accurate because separating the one from the other are fences of barbed wire. Where I was sitting, in full view of the base, I was separated from the nuclear weapons by five fences and entanglements; an outer fence, with barbed wire above and below, then a path, then a barbed wire entanglement, then a third space, and a further barbed wire entanglement, then a much wider space and, in the distance, another fence with its quota of barbed wire.

'We talk of sitting on the fence, but it is not possible to sit on barbed wire, and there is nothing between the devilry and insanity of possessing nuclear weapons, and the joy, and the freedom, and the love, and the glory, and the POWER of the Lord Jesus Christ, the King of all Creation.'

Roger Gray

To be a soldier

To be a soldier,
to fight for peace till war shall end –
this is the conflict
Christ calls you to attend:
to forfeit safety for danger
and then, even stranger,
turn enemy to friend.

To be a soldier
confront more than the human foe;
a greater struggle
the cosmic Christ shall show:
sin must be stripped
from high places;
what scars souls and faces
he bids you overthrow.

To be a soldier
means more than wishing war would cease:
it calls for courage
to bring the poor release,
to enter politics praying
and break rank obeying
the power and Prince of peace.

Think not to weary
or lay your great commission down;
nor crave approval,
nor fear the critic's frown.
Prevail through tears, love with laughter,
risk all and hereafter
receive from Christ your crown.

John L. Bell

Basic Christian Communities

By spontaneous combustion of the spirit

In our time basic Christian communities represent a recovered orthodoxy. The movement did not originate in Latin America and spread elsewhere but, in fact, spread all over the world by spontaneous combustion of the Spirit. Its lineaments were already there in Iona in the 1930s and found expression in family groups. One network in Hungary, which survived underground throughout the Russian occupation, has been in existence since 1948.

Basic Christian communities are modest in their claims. They do not profess to be the form of the true, original Church. They simply claim to represent a form of Church which the Spirit has brought into being at this point in history. They represent 'a way of being a church', no more but no less. They insist on space to make discoveries about how to live the faith in order to understand it. They do this not to replace the traditional Church but that the whole Church, in all its forms, may experience renewal.

They meet in small cells which enable members to get deep in the faith and deep with one another. They are centred on Jesus Christ who is the supreme authority. With them the Bible, worship, analysis of situations and engagements which God's purpose demands, relate vividly to one another.

Ian M Fraser

COMMITMENT

'Follow me'

(A story for six voices – one to read the Bible passages, the others to take the reflections in turn)

Read Mark 1:16–20

'Follow me'
he said – and we did.
We let go of the heavy wet nets,
the tough strands of tarred rope:
our strong hands
were empty – we let go
of all we knew how to do,
our livelihood, our identity –
to follow a dream,
a job description
that no one in their senses
would take seriously.
'Follow me'
he said – and we did.

Read Mark 2:13–17

'Follow me'
he said – and I did.
Tax collecting never made me popular,
but it put a roof over my head
and bread on my table –
bitter bread, because grabbed and grudged.
He invited me to become
no longer dog in the manger,
but host at the feast.
He came right under my roof
sharing my bread
and showing me how to share
with all the rest –
'Follow me'
he said – and I did.

Read Mark 7:25–30

'Go,' he said
'Let the children be fed first –
why should the dogs eat their bread?'
But I would not be turned away:
hoping for healing,
hungry for justice,
I stood my ground and argued:
'In God's household
even the dogs are fed.'

Seeing my faith
he told me to go home
and find my daughter healed.
'Go,' he said – and I did.

Read Mark 10:17–22

'Follow me'
he said, for I had asked him
the next step on a journey
of personal salvation.
He reminded me
of all the good things
I already knew and did.
So nothing was left to do –
I was ready to go.
'Now sell all you have,'
he said. 'Give it away to the poor.'
How could I let go just like that –
lighten the load,
shed my responsibilities,
become someone I did not know –
what would be left?
'Follow me,' he said
but with a heavy heart
I shook my head.

Read Mark 10:46–52

'Come'
he said – and I did,
following his voice
through the crowd on the edge of town.
I needed wait no longer,
my voice had been heard
calling for change,
crying out for a fresh start –
even though it meant
casting off old ways,
no longer the needy person everybody knew.
'Come,' he said
and I saw what God could do.
'Your faith has healed you,'
he told me. 'Now go.'
He never said 'Follow me' –
but, as I could see, there was no other way.

Jan Sutch Pickard

Month 1 Day 29

THE REDISCOVERY OF SPIRITUALITY

What is spirituality?

Spirituality is the oil which fuels the machinery by which we relate to God, to God's world and to God's people.

John L. Bell

That which ultimately moves you – the fundamental motivation of your life.

Kathy Galloway

The true mark of Christian spirituality is to get one's teeth into things. Painstaking service to humankind's most material needs is the essence of spirituality.

George MacLeod

Being spiritual is not the same as being religious. Religion is about what you believe and do. Spirituality is to do with quality; it is a thing of the heart. Religion draws lines. Spirituality reads between them. It tends to avoid definitions, boundaries and battles. It is inclusive and holistic. It crosses frontiers and makes connections. It is characterised by sensitivity, gentleness, depth, openness, flow, feeling, quietness, wonder, paradox, being, waiting, acceptance, awareness, healing and inner journey.

But can't religious people have such qualities? Of course! So can political people. Anyone can be spiritual. Christians should be all three – except 'should' is not a very spiritual word.

Brian Woodcock

The Bible writers never use the word 'spirituality'; they concern themselves with the Holy Spirit, and what s/he is doing in the world; and seem to be more interested in the gifts of the Spirit, and in the fruits of the Spirit – love, joy, peace, patience, and so forth – than in a state of being called 'spirituality'. And so I have always been taught to believe that to be 'spiritual' in the biblical sense was to be seen to be showing forth, in daily life, the fruits of the Spirit – and most particularly the one that, according to Paul, rises above them all – love.

John Harvey

Spirituality describes for me – the attempt to live my daily life continually aware of God's presence in all his Creation, in other people and in the world around me; trying to do my daily work and everyday tasks, whatever they may now be or ever were, in the Spirit of Jesus, in tolerance and goodwill and forgiveness offered; appreciation of nature in all its colour and wonder; knowing how much I fail and how greatly I need and receive forgiveness from God and my fellow human beings; knowing too how much I need support of fellow human beings, Christian and non-Christian alike, and of the Church today, despite all its shortcomings (of which I am part).

Jack Orr

It is of course ultimately a matter of balance. To see spirituality in terms of engagement – with God, with one's inner self, with other people, with the issues of life – over against the tendency, too frequent in contemporary culture, to see spirituality as escape, essentially about self-fulfilment apart from concern with others and the world about us, is not in any sense to diminish the significance either of a regular personal devotion discipline or of the importance, within our own lives, of withdrawing occasionally from the busy-ness and demands of people and situations around us for solitary reflection. Such periods deepen our insights, recharge our batteries, help us, in the words of Richard of Chichester's famous prayer, to know God more clearly, love God more dearly, follow God more nearly … The lack of balance occurs when spirituality is regarded as nothing but prayer and contemplation.

Norman Shanks

Month 1 Day 30

THE THIRTY-FIRST DAY

*(On the 31st day of the month the Iona Community
remembers those of its members who have died.)*

I never wanted to be born

*Written originally for the funeral service of a group of
teenagers who had been killed in a car crash, this meditation is
suitable for similar acts of worship, especially where death has
been sudden and tragic. It should be read slowly.*

I never wanted to be born.

The older I grew,
the fonder I became
of my mother's womb
and its warmth
and its safety.

I feared the unknown:
  the next world,
about which I knew nothing
but imagined the worst.

Yet, as I grew older,
I sensed in my soul
that the womb was not my home for ever.

Though I did not know when,
I felt sure that one day
I would disappear through a door
which had yet to be opened,
and confront the unknown
of which I was afraid.

And then,
it happened.

In blood, tears and pain,
it happened.

I was cut off from the familiar;
I left my life behind
and discovered not darkness but light,
                    not hostility but love,
                    not eternal separation
but hands that wanted to hold me.

(Pause)

I never wanted to be born.

I don't want to die.

The older I grow,
the fonder I become
of this world
and its warmth
and its safety.

Month 1 Day 31

I fear the unknown:
    the next world,
about which I know nothing
but imagine the worst.

Yet as I grow older,
I sense in my soul
that this world is not my home for ever.

Though I do not know when,
I feel that one day
I will disappear through a door
which has yet to be opened.

Perhaps having come so safely through the first door,
I should not fear so hopelessly the second.

John L. Bell

Prayer

Be Thou, triune God, in the midst of us as we give thanks for those who have gone from the sight of earthly eyes. They, in Thy nearer presence, still worship with us in the mystery of the one family in heaven and on earth.

We remember those whom Thou didst call to high office, as the world counts high. They bore the agony of great decisions and laboured to fashion the Ark of the Covenant nearer to Thy design.

We remember those who, little recognised in the sight of men, bore the heat and burden of the unrecorded day. They served serene because they knew Thou hadst made them priests and kings, and now shine as the stars for ever.

If it be Thy holy will, tell them how we love them, and how we miss them, and how we long for the day when we shall meet with them again.

God of all comfort, we lift into Thine immediate care those recently bereaved, who sometimes in the night time cry 'Would God it were morning,' and in the morning cry 'Would God it were night.' Bereft of their dear ones, too often they are bereft also of the familiar scenes where happiness once reigned.

Lift from their eyes the too distant vision of the resurrection at the last day. Alert them to hear the voice of Jesus saying 'I AM Resurrection and I AM Life': that they may believe this.

Strengthen them to go on in loving service of all Thy children. Thus shall they have communion with Thee and, in Thee, with their beloved. Thus shall they come to know, in themselves, that there is no death and that only a veil divides, thin as gossamer.

George MacLeod

Month 1 Day 31

'NEW WAYS TO TOUCH THE HEARTS OF ALL'

The real experts

The opposite of poverty, in the Bible, is not riches, but righteousness, justice. As our choices, over these last six decades or so, have helped to create the great increase in poverty and unemployment in our land, so our choices can actually help to rid our land of them. For we are not, despite what we are sometimes told, helpless before an inexorable fate: there is an alternative; and we need to take courage in both hands and start naming that alternative, and making choices, right now.

A pointer, perhaps, to one fundamental choice we need to make: we need to choose to fight poverty and unemployment, rather than give in to it. And the people best equipped to lead us in this fight (a lesson here that we also need to choose to learn) are not the economists and the politicians, whose credibility in these areas is probably damaged beyond repair, but the real experts in this field – the victims of poverty and unemployment themselves. ATD Fourth World, a French-based movement with a centre near Stirling in Scotland, stresses the element of partnership in the fight against poverty. The founder of the movement, the French Catholic priest Joseph Wresinski, saw poverty as essentially a human rights issue. He wrote: 'Whenever men and women are condemned to live in poverty, human rights are violated. It is our solemn duty to come together to ensure that these rights are respected.'

To choose to work together with the real experts in order to fight poverty and unemployment is not simply a pipe dream. In France, Fr Wresinski was appointed in 1985, as a result of his work, to head up a government initiative in the face of increasing poverty there. The Wresinski report, as it was called, proposed 'an approach to anti-poverty policies that places on record the capacity and willingness of very poor families to take a major part in initiatives aimed at overcoming poverty'.

In local authorities, in business and commercial ventures, in voluntary bodies, yes even in churches, we can choose to become partners with 'the poor' and 'the unemployed'. It will mean self-discipline. It will mean a bit of self-sacrifice – we will not, if we make such a choice, be free also to indulge in all the other choices we might want to make. But if this outrageous and blasphemous assault on the poor is to end, then it is no use at all for us to sit around and blame everyone else from Government down, and refuse to face up to hard choices ourselves. We need to choose to start ending it – now.

John Harvey

ECONOMIC WITNESS

The body was put in a plastic bag

When the World Bank held a conference in Manila in 1976, squatters were displaced. They huddled under makeshift shelters, the children's teeth chattering in the rain. World Banks do not ask about the cost of their visiting. Free paint had been given out so that the appearance of things might be temporarily improved along the routes that cars would traverse.

In 1982, Margaret accompanied me to the Philippines. It was her first visit. We saw one of the effects of holding the SE Asian Games in that country at that time. We were in an area which was deemed to be an eyesore by the authorities. It would disgrace the country if competitors from many nations saw it. So, although the tenants had a legal right to their property and could not be faulted on payment of dues, bulldozers were sent in and their shacks demolished.

Residents were dumped on the outskirts of Manila, including a husband, wife and five children. They had no resources. No work was to be found. They drifted back. The husband, worn out by malnutrition and worry, coughed up his lifeblood. There was no money to bury him. The body was put in a plastic bag and lay around for two weeks. Neighbours at last sacrificially raised enough to secure his burial.

The neighbours then built a lean-to against a wall and covered the framework with plastic (from the bag used for the body) to provide minimal accommodation for the widow and children. Its total extent was about 10' by 4'. A low platform kept the family off the mud and had to serve for beds. Five plastic bags acted as wardrobes for the children's clothes. That had to be home.

When a small boy gently took Margaret's hand and pressed it to his brow, seeking in this way her blessing, she felt all broken up. We felt we should be on our knees before these neighbours, seeking their blessing.

Ian M Fraser

YOUTH CONCERN

Harvest

One Autumn afternoon – after
the night's storm – the ground
in the country field was littered
with green shells and shiny
brown conkers.
We arrived – leaving behind us the
traffic and city streets –
Peter – ready to hurl sticks
Gary – not quite sure if he felt
sick and
Glen – silent and thoughtful.
They found it hard to believe –
as we moved from tree to tree –
there were conkers and conkers and
still more conkers – no need
even to shuffle through the
leaves or prise open tight
shells – just to reach down
and gather them in.
Gary – if Jesus ever told a
true parable about you, it
was that of the farmer who
built more and more barns –

having stuffed your pockets you
proceeded to fill your socks –
till at last you gave in and
turned to climbing the trees.
Glen – not quite believing
it all – asking tentatively if
you could keep some for
yourself –
Peter – helping me fill the
bag – laughing and picturing
Gary taking home enough
conkers to fill his bedroom.
Glen – you made us laugh
when, on hearing the church bells
you asked If ice-cream vans
came out this far into the
country.
In the car home we talked –
laughing as the wind blew
papers all over the back seat –
Glen describing the beautiful
girl he'd marry –
Gary shouting Giddy-up to a
passing horse.
And so we returned home –
back to the maisonettes and the
tower blocks –
having shared in the Autumn harvest.

Ruth Burgess

The ice-cream van

I had an experience which illustrates the pressures young people face, when I was living on an estate with high levels of unemployment and poor housing. I remember noticing how frequently the ice-cream van came, always late at night and surrounded by teenagers. I asked my neighbour about this, and she told me that drugs were sold over the counter. On this housing scheme, young people were living in an environment where drugs were cheaper and more accessible than fresh fruit and vegetables. This is only one story, but it is indicative of the realities of life for some young people.

Rachel McCann, community worker

THE WORD

Revolution as well as revelation

The Bible is about revolution as well as revelation …
The theme of social justice echoes through the pages
of scripture like an insistent drum-beat – from the
Exodus account of the liberation from Egypt, through
the Deuteronomic code with its special concern for
the disadvantaged, the consistent, urgent message of
the prophets, to the life and teaching of Jesus and
Paul's pointing to the perpetual challenge of the
kingdom of God that stands all worldly values on
their head. However marginal an interest in social
and political issues may sometimes seem to the
mainstream of church life …

Norman Shanks

Hospitality and Welcome

The need of the stranger

The hospitality we owe to the stranger who comes among us is well and widely understood. The Old Testament abounds with exhortations to care for the sojourner, the traveller, the person who, by definition, is not 'one of us'. Leviticus 19:34, Exodus 22:21, Deuteronomy 24:17 – these and many more passages urge us to meet the needs of the stranger. 'You shall love the stranger, for you were strangers in the land of Egypt.' The letter to the Hebrews takes up the same theme with its encouragement to welcome the stranger (Hebrews 13:1). We hardly require a second telling to respond to the stranger's need. What we are slow to recognise is our need of the stranger.

The stranger may have an identity, in nationality, colour or creed, that is different from the surrounding majority. For that reason, he or she has the potential for cracking our prejudices, breaking our horizons, disturbing our complacencies. That potential is precarious. People of faith often have exclusive tendencies and none more so than the Jews. Yet the book of Ruth is not only one of the loveliest in the Bible, it is also a special favourite among Jews. It is read in its entirety at the Jewish celebration of Pentecost. Indeed, Ruth holds a position among Jews comparable, we are told, to that which Mary holds among Christians. It is not easy for us to know precisely what Ruth's contribution to her new nation was, but she demonstrates a steadfast loyalty at the personal level. 'Your people shall be my people and your God my God' (Ruth 1:16). These are some of the most strongly ecumenical words in the Bible. No Jew would question Ruth's contribution to Israel's history. Yet Ruth was an outsider; she was a Moabitess; she was one of 'them'. This suggests a truth which we may find uncomfortable. We need the stranger more than the stranger needs us.

Maxwell Craig

THIS IS THE DAY

Benediction of a day

To take a natural analogy, there is a living flower. You want to have it, so you pluck it. But, by your act of plucking, it dies.

You are fascinated by a sparkling running stream, a living stream of water. But, if you grasp it, it runs through your fingers, you scoop it into a pail, you no longer have life, but just a bucket of H_2O.

There is a sunbeam dancing in your room, life from the sun. If you pull down the curtain to capture the beam, it is gone.

There is a bracing wind that enlivens your whole being. But try to catch it in a bag and you have stagnant air. All this reminds us how not to get in touch with life.

Here is the root trouble of our lives. We all love life, but the moment we try to hold it, we miss it. The fact that things change and move and flow is their life. Try to make them static and you die of worry.

This is just as true of God who is the Life of life. The only way to achieve a sense of God's presence is to put yourself in the way of Him. In our analogy, you achieve a sense of life in the presence of a flower, by a running stream, in a bracing wind, with sunbeams falling on the stream. You come home to say you have had a perfectly lovely day, which means a lively day. It has been a benediction of a day.

You can only achieve a sense of God in a similar way. You can only find God in the now.

George MacLeod

Prayer on a given day

(In the Shetland Isles, where folk are used to wind and rain,
an unexpected day of calm sunshine is called a 'given day'.)

Creator God, we thank you for this given day:
for your glory shining forth in sky and sea,
in the changing light on the hills,
in the flight of birds,
in the flowers of meadow and garden
(name birds and/or flowers according to the season)
We thank you for your love experienced in our own lives:
for new friends and old
(by name)
for caring and conversation, for community and solitude,
for work and play, for words and silence
(silence)
We thank you for this gift of time:
may your Spirit help us to use it creatively
in the name of Jesus,
who gave his life to let us know your love. Amen

Jan Sutch Pickard

THE IONA EXPERIENCE

Engagement rather than escape

What brings so many people to Iona is essentially a spiritual journey in search of meaning, purpose and value at a time when so many of the old certainties seem to be breaking down, exposed as inadequate to the tensions, questions and pressures of today, and traditional institutions, the church included, do not fully meet people's needs. 'Celtic spirituality' in particular has a fascination, a curiosity value and attraction because of its perceived association with remote natural beauty and the past, and is often explored in the context of the quest for personal growth that reflects the current individualistic ethos. The Iona Community's understanding of spirituality, however, has to do with engagement rather than the kind of escape that smacks of nostalgia and the romantic. It is founded on the incarnational theology that has characterised the life of the Community since its outset. It asserts that the genuine Celtic tradition of spirituality, as found in the Columban church, had a strong social and communal dimension: God is thoroughly down-to-earth, to be discovered, encountered and experienced not only in personal reflective meditation but also in the practicalities and particularities of life, in human struggles and relationships as much as in tranquillity and the contemplation of natural beauty. 'Spirituality is where prayer and politics meet,' as Kate McIlhagga, a Community Member who is a United Reformed Church minister in the North of England, has said.

Norman Shanks

Life in Community

Iona weaving

How can we comprehend it, God, this beauty and this pain?
How does it hold together?
Is there pattern or purpose?

On a still December day,
warp and weft glimpsed in the gold threads of the dawn sky,
in the blue-grey restless waters of the Sound,
in our laughter and our tears,
in our life together in this place –
your mysterious weaving of the world.

In the battle-song and surge of the waves
    and the living silence of the hills.
In the welter of winter gales
    and the sheltering space of the church or home.
In angry exchanges that unravel,
    and words and spaces that heal.

In isolation and in solitude.
In welcomes at the jetty
    and in saying goodbye.
In the wind-bent trees, blasted by salt
    and flowers flourishing in the village gardens.
In busyness that leaves no time
    and folk making time, here and now.
In the richness of all we have lost.
In discord –
    and in ceilidh music.
stumbling in the dark –
    and dancing under the stars.

How can we comprehend it:
Your beauty and ours – who are made in your image?
Our pain and yours – who chose to share our lives?
We cannot hold it together – but it holds us.

Help us to see pattern and purpose,
    and our part
in the weaving of the world. Amen

Jan Sutch Pickard

WOMEN

Nightmares in the garden

According to the traditional interpretations of Genesis 2–3, the Garden of Eden was a pleasant paradise of sufficiency, security, protection, care, innocence and companionship; until the poison of disobedience and sin seeped in. Then the first human beings were given due punishment: labour and toil for Adam, longing and subjection for Eve. And so the fallen world, tainted with sexual fear, lust and the power of men over women, has become prey to exploitation and violence. Well, that's the story, and it's been imprinted deep onto the minds, hearts and bodies of women and men. But what if that subjection followed from the rationale of Eden itself; and what if that myth, of man and woman; husband and wife; two people, one flesh, eternally united as God and nature intended, has been a basic source of sexual violence?

What characterised the relationship of Adam and Eve in the primal, innocent romance? According to centuries of Christian readings, there were three fundamental elements:

> Eve was created *after* Adam
> Eve was created *from* Adam
> Eve was created *for* Adam

The idea that women were, by divine purpose, derivative and ancillary, enters into the Christian tradition through Paul (1 Corinthians 11), who proposes a hierarchy of order, headship and glory in the image of God. Women reflect the likeness of God, not in themselves, but only through men: 'He for God only, she for God in Him.'[1]

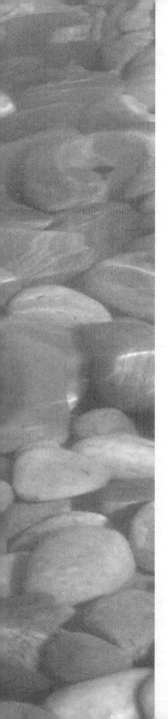

Eve was brought into being not for her intrinsic worth, but to 'help' Adam. She was constructed out of Adam's side, and he assumed the right to name her as such. And what was the point of making her?

The overwhelming consensus of the tradition was that women were, as one seventeenth-century cleric put it, 'vessels for use'. Their original and enduring function was to minister to the requirements and desires of men.

One humanity, two sexes: woman made for man. In Christian theology, sexual duality and complementarity has been presented as the natural order. Only by accepting their radical difference and distinctive functions could men and women fulfil the divine intent. As countless people have discovered to their cost, any departure from this prescribed norm was regarded as deviant and monstrous. Compulsory heterosexuality has proclaimed other modes of sexual expression to be deviant, and therefore subject to censure. Gender complementarity has, historically, declared that women who refused to conform to their prescribed roles in relation to men were monstrous. They dared to step out of the tightly confined and controlled 'women's sphere', and could be chastised accordingly. The branks, a common post-reformation Scottish punishment for 'unruly women', was a painful iron mask which was designed specifically to make the wearer look like a hideous monster. And still, in contemporary Britain, women are confronted with regular reminders that they are alien, unwelcome invaders in male space. There have been alarming cases of sustained sexual harassment and abuse of women in traditionally male environments: the fire service, the police, the Houses of Parliament, the church.

The tyranny of dualism in Western thought and culture has been well documented, especially by feminists. Supported by research in the human sciences of biology and genetics, they argue that the idea of two sharply differentiated sexes is largely a social creation, unsupported by any natural order, and requiring constant vigilance and coercion for its maintenance. It is not difference *per se*, but the way that difference is used to systematise subordination which has normalised the possibility of violence and abuse in gender relations. The story of Adam and Eve, as archetype and model of God's order, has embedded gender dualism in our social and ethical arrangements, by presenting it not as a matter of cultural construction, kept in place by human convention and decision, but as inescapably *natural*, and therefore beyond the scope of human manipulation and revision.

Lesley Orr Macdonald

Woman without a name*

Woman
without a name,
raped and abused
until break of day
then taken limb by limb
through the length of the land.
What symbolism is this?
What do I hear
in your silences?

Who questions your abuse
and the crime
against female sexuality
when the only question is misuse
of man's property?

Can I stand in solidarity
with your pain
and let the silence be
wordless?

Is your silence
louder than the cry
from the cross?

Joy Mead

This poem refers to text in Judges 19

Prayer

The cat and the monkey

Hildegarde of Bingen in the 12th century wrote that spirituality is communal, not simply about the individual's personal relationship with God. Through the centuries it has been our great failure as Christians to privatise our spirituality, for, as Hildegarde writes, Christian spirituality forces our relationships on other people. To be a Christian is to be incorporated into community. She therefore picks up the idea from Jewish theology of two activities which embody spirituality:

'Devekut' or 'clinging to God' – our need for contemplating the Mystery and in it finding our nourishment, and
'Tikkun O' lam' or 'repair of the world' – our responsibility to work for justice and the bringing in of God's Kingdom.

The Benedictine carvings of the cat and the monkey in Iona Abbey also remind us of this balance in our spirituality – activity and contemplation.

Lynda Wright

Prayer

God in the midst, come close to us,
and help us come close to you,
as, for a fraction of time,
we step back from the activities of the day.
May we treasure such moments with you.
Moments when we can bring to you
the things we are doing,
and find new meaning for them,
and new strength for doing them.
And moments for recalling
how we are meeting you already,
in the stuff of daily living and engagement,
when faith is tested
and compassion is translated into action.
So if, as the day goes on, we forget you,
do not forget us, O God.
AMEN.

Brian Woodcock

JUSTICE AND PEACE

But does that mean politics?

It is matter which is at the root of the spiritual, if the Incarnation is to have its central place in our thinking. Our spirituality is tested in how we handle the material. But does that mean politics?

The issue was clarified for me on the Howrah Bridge, Calcutta. A young man was running through the traffic, pulling a rickshaw in which two adults were seated. The sweat poured down his face and his bare feet slapped out a rhythm on the hot, dusty road. He was a beast of burden; our host said he would die at a young age. Elsewhere in Calcutta, poor people died on the pavements.

Many, many people in the world have no home, little food, no money, few clothes, no bed. They die of disease or malnutrition at an early age. The rickshaw wallah pounding the streets of Calcutta, pulling fellow human beings for a few rupees, must make God cry. Of course you 'know' this intellectually; but it is different from seeing, feeling, smelling, touching. And when you look into the eyes of the poor, you become aware of your own complicity.

What to do? Living paralysed by guilt is no great help to the poor. Love demands nothing less than a re-ordering of the world's priorities: a new economic and political order. I can only glimpse what that might mean: part of me is afraid to look any further at the implications. Justice is at the very heart of the faith, not an optional extra. And God's justice in the present situation is transformed into a word of prophetic judgement, whether we like it or not.

Charity is not enough. The work of Mother Teresa in caring for the dying is beautiful – but if nothing is done to change the overall arrangements of a world dominated by the 'Christian' West, the poor will die in the gutters of the Calcuttas of the world for all time.

Prayer is not about turning one's back on all this. Thomas Merton, a Roman Catholic monk who went into a monastery to escape the world, found himself in the silence addressed by a God who cares about the oppressed. Reflecting on the Christian collusion with structures of injustice, Merton pointed out that the Pharisees knew how to arrange things in such a way that the poor would always be with them. We are challenged today to a deeper prayer and a tougher political analysis. If prayer is divorced from the hard-nosed politics of Christian love, it becomes self-indulgent, navel-gazing deep breathing. It will be an abomination to a free God who shouts, 'Take this away from Me!' Politics on its own is not enough, either. If it is uprooted from the forgiving justice at the heart of God, it becomes hard, vengeful, unreformed and ultimately tyrannical.

Justice cannot be separated from peace, any more than prayer can be separated from action. The cost of fuelling the arms race is one million dollars each minute of the day – and while this is going on millions die of malnutrition. The price tag of this kind of 'peace' Is too high and it is being paid in the blood of the poor.

Ron Ferguson

THE INTEGRITY OF CREATION

Dominion

Then God said,
'Let us make humankind in our image,
according to our likeness;
and let them have dominion over the fish of the sea,
and over the birds of the air,
and over the cattle,
and over all the wild animals of the earth.'
(Genesis 1: 26–28)

Dominion, a word which has often been misunderstood, implies caretaking, to act as stewards of God's own purposes. It does not, in its biblical sense, imply the establishment of a competing reign, which is what the fall has led to. Dominion is not domination without justice, but rather responsible rule that does not exploit its charges. God gave instructions to share the earth's vegetation with other creatures (Genesis 1:29–30). The dominion was not God's authority to use up all the earth's resources for human needs alone. A problem in the western world has been that many Christian people have taken God's command of dominion as a divine authorisation to exploit the earth with no thought for the welfare of other cultures, other creatures, the landscape, the mineral resources, the oceans or the atmosphere.

There is no doubt that persuasive and influential misinterpretations of Christian doctrine have led to environmental destruction and lack of respect for nature.

Ghillean Prance

COLUMBAN CHRISTIANITY & THE CELTIC TRADITION

Iona is almost certainly a more exuberantly joyful and relaxed place to be now than it was in Columba's time. The Community bubbles with life and creative energy, its songs proclaiming that 'the life of the world is a joy and a treasure' and inciting us to 'dance and sing, all the earth'.[1] Today there are no gloomy penitentials prescribing punishments for every conceivable lapse. This does not, however, betoken a lack of awareness of or an indifference to the numerous hurts that need to be healed, the sins that need to be forgiven, the wrongs that need to be righted and the disorder and imperfection that needs to be redeemed in the modern world. The Community lives under the shadow of Christ's Cross just as it prays and works under the shadow of the high-standing crosses dedicated to St Martin and St John which dominate the approach to the Abbey. Its joy never slips into triumphalism, nor its relaxed spirit into complacency. It remains uneasy about the deep stain of sin that sullies the world. It is constantly mindful of the presence in our midst of the weak, the vulnerable and the marginalised and names them before God, not with a sigh of resignation or despair but with a sense of determination to work for a better world and hasten the coming of Christ's kingdom. It is this deep spirit of penitence, summed up in the song 'We lay our broken world in sorrow at your feet', which is for me the most authentic mark of the continuing presence of Columban Christianity on Iona.[2]

Ian Bradley

We lay our broken world

(Tune: Garelochside)

We lay our broken world
in sorrow at your feet,
haunted by hunger, war and fear,
oppressed by power and hate.

Here human life seems less
than profit, might and pride,
though to unite us all in you
you lived and loved and died.

We bring our broken towns
our neighbours hurt and bruised;
you show us how old pain and wounds
for new life can be used.

We bring our broken loves,
friends parted, families torn;
then in your life and death we see
that love must be reborn.

We bring our broken selves,
confused and closed and tired;
then through your gift of healing grace
new purpose is inspired.

Come fill us, Fire of God
our life and strength renew;
find in us trust, and hope, and love,
and lift us up to you.

Anna Briggs

Month 2 Day 13

RACISM

What is the challenge to Christians and to the churches?

Last year I phoned a black Christian, active in the church, to ask her to become involved in the movement for change in our immigration laws. After some discussion she said rather sadly that white Christians were not interested in this matter. I asked why. Without hesitation she replied, 'It doesn't happen to them.'

Some years ago I was confronted by a young Muslim woman, very angry at the treatment of Asian women under immigration law. She asked me, a Christian, 'Would you do this to Jesus?'

It does seem to me that something is wrong with us. We have become indifferent, unable to hear, to see, to understand, as Jesus put it. Does Jesus any longer break down the dividing wall? Unless our love for others, our compassion, our thirst for justice are touched and activated by the Spirit we have no answers for these two women. Nor can we rise to this challenge to the integrity of our faith and the integrity of Britain. Yet the gospel is about hope, about change, about loving across barriers of race, about challenging injustice.

As Christians and churches we compromise the gospel. Our theology and experience tell us that racism is a sin, especially when it is sanctioned by the state in legislation. Compromise with that sort of racism means that we shall always be the losers, the gospel always watered down.

Stanley Hope

Prayer

Help us to be an inclusive church.
Christ, unite us in you.
Help us reverse the vicious circle of racism.
Show us how old pains and wounds
can be used for new life…

Yousouf Gooljary-Wright

Month 2 Day 14

COMMUNITY

The WIFOM factor

Our society is in the grip of idolatry. The market is God and the creed is possessive individualism. Of course it is dressed up, given a semblance of respectability, by being presented as personal freedom, enterprise, initiative and the like. But the disguise is not hard to penetrate, and the reality of human selfishness, original sin, is unmasked. There is not necessarily anything intrinsically wrong with the creation of wealth, economic growth, the pursuit of profit, ambition, material success and so on. Getting on is all right – although getting on with other people is more important. The trouble is that our whole culture, for all its glitzy sophistication, seems pretty primitive. Money has become an end in itself rather than simply a means to a higher end; there is a terrible pressure to consume and acquire; it is as if a modern version of the law of the jungle is at work and the weakest are going to the wall. What I think has become known as the WIFOM factor is at work – what's in it for me.

Meanwhile we are told that social justice is a mirage, that poverty is not unfreedom – in the sense, if I understand the argument, that the antithesis of freedom is coercion and people are not coerced into being poor. Such metaphysical stuff is intellectual self-indulgence. Manifestly the trickle-down theory does not work. Providing material incentives for the ambitious, rewarding those who are already well-off does not result in increased philanthropy and beneficence. The mark of a compassionate society is a social policy that is based on mutual caring and equality as well as freedom, that recognises that the elimination of suffering is a public responsibility and cannot be left to private charity.

With increased mobility and the pace we all tend to live and work at we retreat into our little boxes. The experts know more and more about less and less, cultivate their mystique and produce an exclusive in-jargon that keeps out the uninitiated. Communication becomes increasingly difficult; the nuclear family, not even the extended one, far less the community, is the basic unit that matters in people's lives; and in this age of the commuter who knows their neighbour? The emphasis at home, at work, perhaps even at play, is on competition and survival. No wonder there is so much alienation in people's lives. We do not have time even to pay adequate attention to our own deeper needs. And the alienation of the quarter of our society who are left behind in the struggle is extreme.

Norman Shanks

PILGRIMAGE

The pilgrim path

Christians can be described as 'the pilgrim people of God', and in the Bible this idea of the spiritual life as a 'journey' is expressed many times. Through the centuries, pilgrims have come to places like Iona seeking healing, inspiration and redirection.

The outward pilgrimage is a sign of this inner journey – of repentance, resurrection and rebirth – the journey of the heart, held in the Creator's hands. It is rooted in the conviction that life itself is a process of continual change and movement. We are never static, and we carry within us a sense of expectancy, of looking forward in hope.

The writer to the Hebrews framed that reality in some memorable words: 'Therefore, since we are surrounded by so great a cloud of witnesses, let us also lay aside every weight and sin that clings so closely, and let us run with perseverance the race that is set before us, looking to Jesus the pioneer and perfecter of our faith' (Hebrews 12:1–2, NSRV). Here is expressed that marvellous journey of the Christian soul, on a continuing pilgrimage into the heart of God – a pilgrimage which will never be completed here on earth, but continues in God's wider Kingdom.

Iona, in a particular way, is associated with pilgrimage, but the 'pilgrim path' is located everywhere and never just in sacred places. The question remains: are we open to being a pilgrim? Are we prepared to live with some of the risks and uncertainties and loose ends which pilgrimage always entails? The pilgrim can never have everything neatly 'sewn up' – there is always the exploration, the search, the movement, the questions and the challenge.

Each Wednesday there is a pilgrimage round the island, visiting places of historical and religious significance and reflecting on the journey of our lives and the life of the world. Yet whether on a Hebridean island or in our homes, Christ keeps inviting us to join him on this journey into Light and Truth.

Peter Millar

At Columba's Bay
they met;
two of Iona's
countless pilgrims.
He, a pastor from Zaire;
she, a broker from Detroit.
And battered by the
autumn wind and rain
they shared their stories –
twentieth-century stories –
rooted in contrasting realities,
yet both embedded
in a strange, life-giving
brokenness.
The hidden stories –
of poverty and torture,
of cancer and loneliness;
interweaving stories,
mirroring our
global interconnectedness.
And stories of faith;
of God's unfolding
in their lives
through ordinary days.
And suddenly it seemed
that for a moment
on that distant shore
they glimpsed
that basic truth –
that truly
we are one
in Christ.

Peter Millar

Month 2 Day 16

SEXUALITY

All the parts of the body

During Community Week on Iona, a group of mostly young Abbey and MacLeod Centre staff volunteers planned and led an evening service on the theme of gay and lesbian sexuality.

The liturgy, which had arisen out of their concern, offered up to God in repentance and sorrow the exclusion, persecution and even death suffered by gay and lesbian men and women in many places and at many times. And in a litany of celebration, those present were invited to remember and give thanks for those gays and lesbians whose lives had graced the world. The names of many famous writers, artists, musicians, sportsmen and women, politicians, philosophers, philanthropists were read out ... Tchaikovsky, Bernstein, Whitman, Auden, Virginia Woolf, Eleanor Roosevelt ... the list went on. The congregation was asked to add the names of people they themselves knew.

Then something extraordinary happened. Names came from all parts of the church – so many that when the leaders thought they were finished, they had to begin again. And people began to give not just names but testimony, speaking of friends, relatives, sons and daughters dearly loved and celebrated, often in the face of great hostility and prejudice. It was as if something had been released, and a silence had been broken. Gay and lesbian men and women had come into the house of God and been named, not in condemnation or pity, but in celebration, as full members of the human body ...

Loving sexual relationship is a constellation of experiences, feelings and struggles. It is intimacy and humour, respect and care, making a home, sharing ideas and having arguments. It is the ordinary things of life with the thread of bodily relaxation and familiarity running through it. To withdraw the possibility of partnership from gay and lesbian men and women is to deny them far more than just sex.

And if I am not fully human, if I am seen to be defective or disordered in some intrinsic way, then signals are given that it is possible to treat me in other ways which my less than fully human status allows for – to insult me, to dismiss me from my job, to limit my civil and political rights, to attack me with physical and psychological violence, to jail me, perhaps even put me in a concentration camp and gas me. Less often remembered is the fact that tens of thousands of people were murdered by the Nazis precisely because they were homosexual.

I am called in Christ not only to be in solidarity with gay and lesbian Christians but to work at what it means to be in solidarity with those who openly consider my kind of Christianity to be 'the enemy'. But even more, it is to consider my own part in the wounding, the places where I have not listened, or listening have not heard, or hearing have not acted in concern for the wellbeing of *all* the parts of the Body (Gal. 3:28).

Kathy Galloway

Dancing on the edge

You take one step forward and three steps back,
you're not sure of the rhythm and it's confidence you lack
for you fear that on this journey you will leave the beaten track
but you're dancing, you're dancing on the edge.

Your family have abused you so from now on you're all alone;
the doorways of the city are the place you call your home;
and you really do not know if you can make it on your own,
so you're dancing, you're dancing on the edge.

The baby wakes you screaming and you don't know what to do;
the giro's almost finished, but all the bills are due
and there's no one that you trust, no one you can turn to
and you're dancing, you're dancing on the edge.

You've fled from persecution and you want to find some peace;
but they've put you in a prison and you can't get your release
and you know they'll send you back to face the secret police,
for you're dancing, you're dancing on the edge.

The pain you feel inside is too much for you to bear,
so you turn to drink and drugs to find some comfort there,
and the only human contact is the needle that you share
as you're dancing, you're dancing on the edge.

When the church will not accept you because they know you're gay
and the righteous congregation all turn their face away,
and you wonder who their God is when they're kneeling down to pray
and you're dancing, you're dancing on the edge.

When they've pushed you to the limit and you feel you can't go on;
rejected and reviled and your hope has almost gone:
in Jerusalem, this happened to God's only precious Son
as he was dancing, dancing on the edge.

Sometimes together, sometimes far apart;
to love or martial tune, we each must make a start;
sometimes, quite simply, to the rhythm of His heart,
we're dancing, we're dancing on the edge.

Alix Brown

Month 2 Day 17

HEALING

All healing is of God

Healing is a central obligation of the Church. Christ came neither to save souls nor to save bodies. He came to save people. Thus our whole ministry is one of healing: making the crooked places straight in international issues, in class issues, and issues of sex. In Christ Jesus there is neither Jew nor Greek, bond nor free, male nor female. He is the At-one-ment. And as of the larger, so of the less. Christ makes crooked people straight. As in the body politic, so in the human body. He makes straight, here the crooked mind and there the crooked body, and most often the crooked mind-body.

Just as there is no such thing as 'Christian truth' over against truth, so there is no such thing as 'Christian healing' over against healing. All healing is of God, and the man who walks again after penicillin is just as much divinely healed as a man who walks again after a service of laying-on of hands. We have no divine repository where 'religious' things happen over against a hospital where so-called merely physical things happen.

We must avoid the danger of 'separateness' – the tendency to concentrate on divine healing as if it can be an isolated recovery, sealed off from social concern. It comes, for instance, somewhere near blasphemy that we should merely pray for 'Margaret suffering from TB' when we know quite well this illness was contracted in a damp room in the slums of Glasgow. This is not to say that we dare not pray for Margaret till all the slums are cleared. For God is a father, and not just an indifferent guardian of righteousness. He is a God of mercy who saves and heals, while we are yet sinners. But it is to say that it is near blasphemy merely to pray for her individually when there is a known cause which we should be tackling at the same time.

George MacLeod

Prayer

Watch now, dear Lord,
with those who wake or watch or weep tonight,
and give your angels charge over those who sleep.
Tend your sick ones, O Lord Christ,
rest your weary ones,
bless your dying ones, soothe your suffering ones,
pity your afflicted ones, shield your joyous ones,
and all for your love's sake.
Amen.

And now may the God of hope
fill us with all joy and peace in believing,
that we may abound in hope
in the power of the Holy Spirit
Amen.

(The Iona Abbey Worship Book)

Month 2 Day 18

SOCIAL ACTION

Put your money where your mouth is!

George MacLeod said that there was little point in just praying that someone who was ill would get better if we don't do something about the damp house which has made them ill in the first place.

In a similar vein, there can be little point in praying for justice and peace if we do nothing about where it really counts: through our purchasing power. If we continue to buy goods which have been made by companies whose hidden byword is exploitation, then we really are praying pretty hollow prayers.

Through the policy of Fair Trading we can be sure that the gifts and goods we buy are helping those whose needs are so often ignored: the people in the poorest parts of the world who make the commodities we take for granted.

Adrian Rennie

CHURCH RENEWAL

We would rather do it with you

The only reason I had decided, finally, after a long struggle, to become a minister was that I believed that other people were the church.

There was one night that the theology group met and we were doing various very worthwhile pieces of work but the idea of developing the centre had begun to emerge, and I was pretty scared by the whole thing. I think I probably recognised how enormous and how apparently unrealistic the project was, and so I suggested to the group that it was perhaps too big an undertaking, and that we should go back to doing the small things that we'd been doing beforehand. And one member of the group said, 'Well, Martin, we believe this is what God wants us to do. And we're going to do it, and we're going to do it with or without you. But we would rather do it with you.'

And at that point I had to recognise that I probably had the power to stop it from happening – but if I did I should probably leave the church, for my reason for being there would be a sham.

Martin Johnstone

WORSHIP

Worship renews life
A service in an Indian village, Guatemala

The church was packed. Men and women occupied separate sides. It was the women who did most of the singing. That day, for the first time ever, two women also read from the Old Testament and the Epistle. The priest had the custom of wearing informal clothes up to the point where the service was ready to start, then putting on a cassock and stole (of local embroidery) in front of the people, removing them immediately the service ended. It made clear that the special dress did not denote membership of a different caste; rather that the worship was led by a specially appointed representative, whose function began and ended with the service.

In front of the church on the right was a black Christ on a cross, balanced on the other side by a white Virgin Mary. There were flowers, there were saints and symbols, and, in the centre, a kind of box-tent for the reserved sacrament. The reading was on the Good Samaritan.

The sermon was a dialogue with the people. At one point they were asked if they felt assaulted as was the Jew in the story. 'Yes,' they said. 'By what?' asked the priest. 'By illness,' one said. The main attack on the life of the community, they said, came by way of the river. The village was built on both sides of an almost-dry gorge which had been adopted by the city of Guatemala, without consultation with the people, as a sewage outlet.

The people saw the gospel as an invitation to get to grips with this situation and to fight to change it. Mention was made of the latest priest to be killed and the people calmly faced up to the realisation that they were called to live as God's children, transforming life, even if that meant the risk of death.

The prayers which followed came from the congregation, a good number of men and women participating. The peace was given, hand on one another's shoulders. All adults received the communion.

Prayer

Pray that
The gift of worship may be so appreciated as to become
fundamentally renewed wherever it grows stale;
The endowments of the Spirit, distributed among all,
may not be quenched but released so that worship
becomes rich and dynamic;
Rooting in God may lead to fruiting in the world.
Ask this in the name of him who is the Way, the Truth, the Life.
Amen

Ian M Fraser

WORK

Industrial mission

At San Martin, near Barcelona, people from basic Christian communities asked me about Selly Oak, Birmingham. I told them of the nearness of Longbridge, the Austin motors works down the road. They were immediately interested and asked me when there was a dispute at the works how the churches in that locality reacted. Did they mainly take the side of the workforce or of the management? I had to confess that they took very little direct interest as congregations in any industrial dispute.

'Oh, come on,' they said, 'we know that there will be different reactions in different circumstances. Most times we need to side with the workforce. When there is a dispute there is usually some real injustice at the root of it and the workforce are those who take the brunt. There are times when we should side with the management because they seem to have a point which the workforce are a bit blind to. In each case, one of our jobs, as Christians, is to keep the one side open to the other. If you take the side of the shop-floor workers, your identification with them includes the business of communicating to them something which belongs to the management's view of things. If you believe that the management are in the right, you encourage them to appreciate how the shop-floor workers are placed, and how they are reacting. But you always need to take sides and not sit on the fence.

'Of course, there has to be a good foundation from which to act. You have to build up an understanding of the development of industry in your area over a period of many years. It takes time and energy. All that we are asking is whether the churches in the area of Longbridge usually come out on the side of the workforce or of the management.'

I had to repeat my point about the Church's indifference.

They shook their heads, incredulous. 'How can people claim to be Christians and stay out of such things?' they asked.

Ian M Fraser

CALLED TO BE ONE

All things in Christ

The Community's ecumenical commitment, as much as our concern for social and political change, is a natural outworking of the incarnational theology that sees spirituality as engagement and connectedness. It stems from our understanding of the vision and values of God's kingdom and the imperative to respond positively and play a creative part wherever there are signs of hope and growth, as the kingdom breaks through. If the Church is truly a sign and the first fruits of the reconciliation of all things in Christ then our divisions represent a betrayal of our nature and calling, and anything other than a strong commitment to unity is to commit the enormity of dismembering the body of our Saviour in terms of the insights and language of the first chapter of the First Letter to the Corinthians.

Norman Shanks

MISSION

God's sphere of activity is the world

… On the whole I am not enthusiastic or even hopeful about what appear to be the priorities and prevailing views about mission in today's churches.

The concern with church numbers is understandable, especially in a culture accustomed to measuring success and appraising value in quantifiable terms and when so many congregations are struggling both to meet their financial commitments to their local and national denominational headquarters and to maintain their buildings, the cherished heritage of a proud past but no longer suitable to contemporary needs. But the result is a preoccupation with church growth, as if the Church and the kingdom were one and the same; and too often mission is a not very well concealed recruitment drive or, worse still, the promotion of a package. God works through the Church to be sure, and the calling of the Church to fulfil its vocation as an embodiment or foretaste of the kingdom is well established and hard to live up to. The congregation thus has an essential role in the missionary process as channel or agent of the good news but it is not the be-all and end-all as long as the primary emphasis is on building not the Church but the kingdom, seeking to make God real to people where they are. God's purpose and promise are not limited to the Church, for God's sphere of activity is the world, of which the Church is but a part. Mission belongs to God, not to the Church; and the missionary task is thus to discern and point to the signs of the kingdom breaking through wherever this is happening, as it does both within and outside the Church, with church growth a possible and desirable by-product. Mission is about conversation rather than conversion; about engagement, interaction and dialogue rather than verbal persuasion, for the language of action and the witness of integrity and consistency carries more authenticity and credibility than slick words delivered hit-and-run style …

Mission must be focused on the world but centred on God, Jesus Christ, the Gospel and the kingdom, not on the Church; it must reach out unconditionally to proclaim the love of God without seeking to prescribe or even measure the response.

Norman Shanks

THE POOR AND DISADVANTAGED

The gospel is about good news to the poor, liberty to the captives, justice for the oppressed. That is essentially political. If we see real poverty in our inner cities, young people whose sense of worth is steadily eroded by lack of work, the deliberate running down of all our industries, and the systematic destruction of all that constitutes a caring society, then as Christians it is our duty to take action. Christianity affirms the infinite value before God of every individual, and the gospel talks of 'abundant life' in Christ.

Helen Steven

Prayer

Lord God, you humble me before the poor.
The more I have the more I want to cling to.

Jesus Christ did not grasp at divine equality but laid aside his glory,
stripping himself of privilege and security
to live life with the conditions we live under.

He was a vulnerable child, unprotected from Herod's wrath, a refugee;
he was found alongside the lowest, the least, the lost,
he gave all, even life itself.
Yet I hesitate to part with some of my abundance.

Lord God, you humble me before the poor
who when they have a little to eat, share it,
who will fight to secure others' good,
who, having nothing, yet seem to possess all things.

What must I do to be saved?
If we all become poor, there would not even be a portion for each.

I cringe away from the sacrifice Jesus asked of the rich young man.
But I also believe I am not called to part with my possessions as he was.
Or am I? Search my heart; you know my innermost thoughts.

Teach me so to handle the possessions you have entrusted to me
that whatsoever is asked of me,
they will be treated as yours, not as my own.

Teach me grace to give whatever you require of me,
and grace to refuse whatever mistaken pressures guilt would exact from me;

Teach me to fight unjust systems which rob people
of their share of God's provision;

Teach me to be alert to rationalisations and evasions in my own life
and in Church and in public life;

Teach me not to want to keep the poor in poverty
as a sign and reminder to others,
as if merely by being poor they formed a saving remnant.
May I respond to Mary's vision – of the poor lifted high.

All this I ask in Jesus Christ's name and for his sake.

Amen.

Ian M Fraser

INTERFAITH

Sharing Communion

I learned by many experiences in India how God was present in all religions. I was on a bus on a hot-weather journey from Ajmer to Jaipur – about 80 miles. Dozing in the heat I slowly realised the bus had stopped outside a wall in open desert country. It was a temple. The bus conductor alone alighted and I thought, 'Maybe he is visiting a friend.' Sure enough, he was back in a few minutes and drove on without a word. Suddenly I realised I was in a communion service. The people in front of me, Hindu, Sikh, Muslim, had their hands held out and the conductor was giving them a pinch of coconut and sugar – the Prasad. Fortunately, I had time to see what was happening and have my hands out also, when my turn came – the only foreigner, and perhaps the only Christian. No words were spoken, no religion mentioned. We all knew that this bus conductor had ushered us into God's presence, that God had accepted us – each one – and enabled us to accept each other, as we were. No orthodox religion can enter this realm. For instance the Christian religion has plenty to say about things offered to idols. Was he ordained? There we go again!

George More

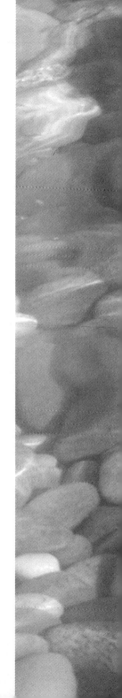

NONVIOLENCE AND PEACEKEEPING

Swords into ploughshares

'But it's individual – you know, if we turned our swords into ploughshares, our tanks into tractors, all nations together, we could without putting a penny on the income tax give a square meal every day to everyone in China, in Africa, in India, and in South America. Presently, we spend, as a nation, 80 millions a year on aid to the underdeveloped countries. But we spend over 2,000 millions on armaments.

Must we go on with this madness? One Polaris carries in its belly the accumulated fire power of all the explosions made by both sides through the whole of the last war.

But no, the world goes on much the same. We begin to behave like computers. We carry on with our heavy tasks. 'I'm all right Jack, what has it got to do with me, anyway?'

How are we going to lift the sights of the Western world to think of other countries than our own? How are we going to convince people that the East is forever getting poorer and the West is forever getting richer, and there will be an explosion one day, and God will be in favour of the other side. It's only for Christ's sake that people will ever be moved. And this is what the Church must be at.'

George MacLeod

God's agenda

Our social values, social goals and social priorities need constantly to be examined from the perspective of the Gospel. How can we claim to be a civilised, caring society when the gap between the richest and the least well-off has been growing wider and wider? Bearing in mind the theme of justice that is a consistent imperative through the pages of scripture, a priority in the life and teaching of Jesus, how can we rest easy with the systematic dismantling and emasculating of our public services and the insidious culture of contentment and possessive individualism which has us all in its grip? This is why we in the Iona Community, along with so many other concerned groups inside and outside the church, are continuing to work for change – standing alongside the poor and the exploited … pressing for reductions in the arms trade and the abandonment of Trident, campaigning against cuts in overseas aid and against increased restrictions on immigrants and asylum-seekers. Yes, this is a political agenda; but it is God's agenda, because no area of human activity is beyond the scope of God's grace and the reach of God's judgement.

Norman Shanks

BASIC CHRISTIAN COMMUNITIES

Life shared
Indian Christian communities In Guatemala
From an interview

It is in the very nature of basic Christian communities that every community has its own special character. They are not clones. Of the seven hundred groups that are in Waiwaitenango, Guatemala, there are seven hundred different kinds. So it would be very difficult to say that there is a model or type which you could label as standard. The exception, however, is that in the Altiplano area of Guatemala, they are all based on Indian culture and on the Indian concept of society. They are Indian communities which get together in an Indian manner, pray in an Indian way, celebrate faith in an Indian way; and members help one another, develop mutual support, in an Indian way. Each basic Christian community in Guatemala would be quite distinctive in the way it expresses its life, while still showing marks of kinship with those in other parts of Guatemala and the wider world.

For example, in a village, when it is time to thatch a roof, all the members of the community get together to help with that roof. It becomes a form of celebration; and through working together they are creating community. The raw material of community can be found when people get together to perform a task such as sowing a seed or thatching a roof; as in the United States during the time of the early colonies when they had quilting bees. The women of the community would get together to make a quilt. That quilt became a symbol of the community. So the thatched roof on the house is a symbol of community or the crop that's about to be harvested is a symbol of community. When you take into consideration that corn is the staple food for many people, the crop that they sow and harvest is a symbol of all that their community is and all that they hope it will be. It is a very powerful symbol.

In that way, in an Indian way, the Indians celebrate community and form basic Christian communities in a way very different from what people in the city would do. Urban people have a different type of culture. Kinship of these two types with one another comes from their being products of one Spirit.

Ian M Fraser

COMMITMENT

Going under

Peter called to him: 'Lord, if it is you, tell me to come to you over the water.' 'Come,' said Jesus. Peter got out of the boat and walked over the water towards Jesus. But when he saw the strength of the gale, he was afraid; and beginning to sink, he cried, 'Save me, Lord!'
(Matthew 14:28–30)

Personnel: *Jesus*
             Peter

            (Peter is evidently embarrassed)

Jesus: Peter ... ?

Peter: *(No response)*

Jesus: Peter ... ?

Peter: *(No response)*

Jesus: Is it as bad as that?

Peter: Mm-hm.

Jesus: But you've changed your clothes ...
             you're dry now.

Peter: It wasn't getting wet that bothered me.
           It was making such a fool of myself.
           Why did you let me do it?
           Surely you knew what would happen?

Jesus: What have the others said?

Peter: They've been quite good actually,
           apart from Andrew
           who keeps making snide comments about webbed feet.

Jesus: Well, your shoulders are broad enough.

Peter: It's not my feet or my shoulders, Jesus,
           it's my head.
           Whatever made me try it?

Jesus: Well, you tell me …
           Why did you try it?

Peter: Oh, you know what I'm like.
           I take these daft notions …
           I always want to be in on the act
           and you made it look so easy.

           We all thought it was a ghost at first.
           I mean, treading grapes is one thing,
           but walking on the water is out of the question.

           Then we realised it wasn't a ghost.
           It was you …
           and you were walking on the sea.

Month 2 Day 29

Jesus: And you wanted to do the same … eh?

Peter: Yes, I did.

Jesus: Why, Peter?

Peter: A bit of me wanted to see if I could do it …

Jesus: And a bit of you wanted to show off … eh?

Peter: Yes … yes, that's right.
            But I did mange it at first, didn't I?

Jesus: Yes you did …
            for about five yards.
            And then … ?

Peter: After that I don't remember a thing
            until I woke up in the boat
            with James pulling seaweed out of my mouth.

            What happened?

Jesus: I'll tell you what happened.
            You stopped looking at me
            and started looking at the waves.

Peter: I could hardly do anything else.
            There was a big swell.

Jesus: Remember Lot's wife, Peter.

Peter: Did she try walking on water?

Month 2 Day 29

Jesus:	No … but like you, instead of looking ahead,
	she began to get fascinated
	by the danger all around her …
	and she ended up being destroyed.

Peter:	I'm not sure of what you're saying.

Jesus:	Peter, I've asked you to follow me.
	And you can only follow me
	if you watch what I'm doing
	and see where I'm going.

	And wherever I am,
	there will be trouble and opposition.
	There will be threats all around you
	and there will be distractions inside you …
	doubt …
	uncertainty …
	and all the old temptations
	you thought you'd left behind.

	If you keep your eye on these things,
	you'll go under.

	If you keep your eye on me,
	you'll stay afloat.

Peter:	Is it as easy as that?

Jesus:	No, Peter.
	It's not as easy as that.
	It's not easy at all.

Peter: Do you ever feel like giving up on me, Jesus?

Jesus: No.

Peter: *(After a moment)*
           … Anything else?

Jesus: Yes …
           it's high time you learnt how to swim.

John L. Bell & Graham Maule

THE REDISCOVERY OF SPIRITUALITY

A liberation theology story

The story of the Orbiston Neighbourhood Centre is one of innovation, energy and success as a community project.

Orbiston is a housing scheme in Bellshill, near Glasgow, which has suffered from sectarian divisions, and economic difficulties following the decline of heavy industry. The Neighbourhood Centre was established to find ways to bridge these divides and to offer mutual support in the face of unemployment and disadvantage.

The approach taken was based on the principles of liberation theology – a methodology of change and empowerment which originated in Latin America and for the first time has been explored in a thorough way in Scotland. Liberation theology starts with people and not dogma, with experience and not theory. Within this context church traditions are explored to discover what they can offer people rather than simply being imposed from above.

This has succeeded in Orbiston by bringing people together in an ecumenical way, healing wounds of separation while acknowledging difference of denomination. The Good Samaritan's challenge to 'love thy neighbour' has been enacted by ordinary people becoming involved in the decisions of local and national government which affect their daily lives, such as the policy of Care in the Community. Feelings of apathy and helplessness have been challenged by mutual support, prayer and accountability, in a creative and imaginative way …

One of the quite unusual features of this story is that it introduces an idea that is more familiar to us (if, indeed, it's familiar at all) from other parts of the world, particularly from the Third World. Liberation theology is a term first used by the Brazilian theologian Gustavo Gutierrez. It involves reading the Bible from the perspective of the poor and dispossessed, encouraging them to see themselves as the subjects of their own life rather than as the objects of other people's understanding of them (whether that understanding be one of pity or of contempt). It is inspired by the great narratives of the Bible, particularly the story of Exodus (the liberation of the Jewish people from oppression in Egypt, hence the term 'liberation'), by the prophetic calls for justice of the Old Testament, and by Jesus's proclamation of the kingdom. It has struck deep chords in places where structures of injustice and economic dependence oppress great numbers of people (as the Gospel indeed did among the poor and oppressed of Jesus's own time, and in many eras since). From it is derived the notion of the 'bias to/preferential option for the poor'.

As much as a theory, liberation theology is a methodology, a way of doing things, a process. It enquires about justice, and does its theology not in a university or church context, but out of the experience of engagement in the public arena, whether that be the street or the factory, the marketplace or the parliament. Its basic model is that of *praxis*, meaning 'to do' – that is, its reflection, study and prayer arises out of its practical engagement, its doing, and not out of theorising. This reflection in turn sets the context for further action, and so on, in an ongoing process of action/reflection/action. The truth of an idea or belief is not based on whether it is intellectually justifiable or doctrinally pure, but by whether it brings about transformation in the lives of persons and communities, and in the structures that shape their lives.

Orbiston is, in Scottish terms, a poor area. Both Orbiston and St Andrew's Churches made a conscious decision to follow the methodology of liberation theology in their attempt to discover what it meant to love their neighbours. Again, it is important to stress that this was not some obscure theory. For them, it was a way of reading the Bible, of praying, of sharing deeply and self-critically in reflection on their own very practical, indeed often mundane action. It is not a political agenda or blueprint – but it proved to have political and economic implications.

Kathy Galloway

The Thirty-First Day

To die healed

(from a reflection on contemporary medicine by Tom Gordon, Hospice Chaplain at the Marie Curie Centre, Edinburgh, and adviser on spiritual care to Marie Curie Cancer Care)

A miner all his days, Bobby was 72 years old and he was dying of lung cancer. He was admitted to our hospice for control of his pain, but it quickly became clear that this was likely to be a 'continuing care' admission, as Bobby was a very sick man. And we realised that he was not going to be an easy man to work with, such was his aggression and uncooperative nature. Bobby had done little to endear himself to the nursing team during the first 24 hours of his admission. When I met him, he was on his own in one of our sitting-rooms, crumpled in a big easy-chair. He looked grey, and he was puffing on a very thin roll-up cigarette. 'Hello, my name's Tom and I'm the Chaplain here. How're you doing?' I said, offering my hand. He took it – reluctantly – and pronounced, 'You'd be as well buggerin' off, son. There's nae point in talkin' tae me. See, 'am a Marxist and an atheist masel'.' If I'd been quick enough, I'd have said something clever like, 'Well, you'll get a prize for getting one right out of two!' But I didn't. I simply said, 'I just wanted to say hello. I'll catch you another time.' And, in all honesty, I hoped I wouldn't have to bother.

The next day there was a message for me: 'Bobby wants to see you – in the sitting room – at ten o'clock sharp!' I was intrigued. So I met Bobby for a second time. 'Aye, right son, come in. Sit yersel' down.' (As if it was his front room.) 'Now, how long've you got? 'Cos I dinnae want ye tae run away. I want tae tell ye ma life story.'

And he did! – from the age of 13 when he first went down the pit to supplement the meagre income of a large, fatherless family, through years of capitalist exploitation, Union politics, family stresses, picket-lines, drink, fags, religion, friendships, the prospect of death, the lot. It took him an hour and a half. Exhausted, he sank back in his chair. There was a long silence. Then he said: 'Well, son, what do you make o' that? Has ma life been any good?'

At that moment I was at the sharp end of spiritual care, because a craggy old atheist miner was asking a spiritual question – of someone with whom he would never agree in religious terms, but whom for his own reasons he trusted with his sixty-four-thousand-dollar question in the face of death.

'Yes,' I replied, 'your life's been good, right enough. A life's work for better conditions for miners? That'll do for me.'

Bobby died three days later, and with greater peace and considerably less anger than he showed on admission. More people than me played their part in that. But I know Bobby was on a spiritual journey, sorting things out before he died, 'finishing the business', concluding a search for meaning, purpose, fulfilment, seeking an affirmation of the worth of his life. And Bobby found healing in his search.

Tom Gordon

'New Ways to Touch the Hearts of All'

Beauty beyond words

The Camas Centre lies at the end of a two-mile track which traverses drainage ditches, peat bog, low-growing heather, ubiquitous bracken, and bog myrtle forest. Old stone dykes flank much of the track before it rises to unveil the wonder of Camas Bay, with its distinct tidal island. The old fishing cottages seem as if they are sliding into the sea; and from the rise in the track, one can see the severity of the Ardmeanach cliffs. It was from here that a young guest from a residential school, a young man very nervous about arriving in a place so different from his native Glasgow, proclaimed, 'It's so beautiful.'

The land itself seemed to provoke wonder in young people visiting the centre on week-long retreats. After this young man affirmed nature's 'beauty beyond words', I always paused at the rise in the track while leading groups to the Centre. Often I perceived the hard shells of these young people crack under a beauty which transcends class, history, even understanding.

Eric Wojchik (Camas programme worker)

> Originally quarry-workers' cottages, then a salmon-fishing station, the Camas Centre on the Isle of Mull is run by a staff group with specialist skills, helped by several volunteers. Young people from the city and

elsewhere, and other groups too, come to Camas for an adventure holiday with outdoor opportunities for canoeing, walking, swimming and camping, a visit to Iona, and the experience of exploring issues, building relationships, and facing new challenges through living and working in community.[1]

(from *What is the Iona Community?*)

ECONOMIC WITNESS

The way in the world
The economic discipline of the Iona Community

'Either Christ is the Lord of all, or he is not Lord at all.'

The Iona Community, it could be said, has always been about two things in particular. It has been about the whole Gospel for the whole world: in George MacLeod's words, 'Either Christ is the Lord of All, or he is not Lord at all.' And secondly it has been about trying out, together, ways of living this total Gospel – experimenting, following a way while finding one, seeking 'new ways to touch the hearts of all'.

One of the areas of life it began experimenting in from a very early stage was that of money – economic witness. For over fifty years, this area of our common life has probably been the most testing and demanding of all: and today we are still struggling with it as hard as ever. Because it is still as central as ever to our conviction, that Christ is the Lord of All.

To set the Community's experiment in economic discipline in its proper context, we need to begin not with the Iona Community at all, but with common biblical faith.

God's revelation to Moses was as the One who sought a covenant relation-ship with the chosen people in total terms: worship of body, mind and spirit, and right relationships with each other in material terms (in the family, with the neighbours, in regard to property, for instance) – these were the commandments of Jehovah. Through the prophets, God's revelation was as the One who simply would not tolerate the lip service of a purely spiritual religion – 'Stop your noisy songs; I do not want to listen to your harps; instead let justice flow like a stream, and right relationships like a river that never goes dry.' Unheeding, the Israelites built bigger and better temples, and sang louder and louder songs; nor did they listen much better when John came, baptising and preaching repentance, and showing them that the fruits of repentance were to be seen in material terms.

Then came Jesus: proclaiming the Year of Jubilee; healing bodies as well as souls; and so infusing with the spirit the common material things of life – bread, wine, wood, nails, thorns, water, blood – that his early followers, the slaves and the freedmen and women of the Roman Empire, similarly infused, practised a lifestyle of simple communism, in which, with apparent naturalness (but, as we know, by grace alone!) their sharing was total indeed – 'They had all things in common.'

The Church – and the world – has come a long way since then. And, at least in the West, while God has never left us without some to witness to the totality of the Gospel's promise and the Gospel's demands, it seems we have come to terms, both in the world and in church, with division and with partiality.

So it is that we 'don't talk about money' in the Church.

So it is, paradoxically, that the common accusation is that 'the church is always on about money'. (Which arises, surely, from the undeniable fact that, when the Church does talk about money, it usually means money for itself.)

So it is that the only people in the Church who are placed by the Church under any sort of 'economic discipline' are its paid servants!

And, finally and most desperately, so it is that the Church is not seen to have anything credible to say about the present economic chaos of the world – the same world which we proclaim, in sermon, hymn and prayer, to be 'the world God loved so much that he sent his only begotten Son'.

The response of the Iona Community to this biblical faith and this churchly failure, so briefly summarised above, has been twofold.

First, we have said *Mea Culpa*! It's our fault; we are sinners; we are as guilty as any of the Church's failure in this area of economic witness.

Then, second, we have kept on saying, 'Christ is the Lord of all!' Therefore, we have said, gritting our teeth and urging each other on, that by grace alone we will seek to be responsive to Christ's Lordship of all, by trying to let him be Lord of the economic too. And we will start in the only place we can: in the personal, so that when it comes to the political, as come it must, we may be seen to have something credible to say.

Today, we do it like this. In our small family groups, we account to each other for the total use of our net income. This accounting to each other, as Ralph Morton said, is one of the great strengths of our scheme. It may sound threatening, but it is in fact supportive. It is never easy, but done properly it offers great ease of spirit; and it keeps you at it, instead of letting you off the hook with pious words and good intentions.

Then, annually, we agree, again in our family groups, on what are to be our individual base-line commitments, and any special circumstances and expenses; and thus arrive at a personal disposable income figure for each of us, from which a tithe (10% in most cases) can be deducted.

All members of the Iona Community are committed to this scheme. Most would confess that they find it demanding; some would wish it were different; some, too, would like it to be a fuller scheme, and less of a token one. On the whole, however, it has undoubtedly received the support of hundreds through the years; and it has spilled over into the Associates, who have a similar, although purely voluntary, scheme of economic discipline. It is only a start: we do not claim that it is a solution for the economic chaos of our times; what we do claim is that it is a response, in economic terms, and in a disciplined way, to biblical revelation that Christ is the Lord of all.

John Harvey

Prayer

Eternal God,
out of your great generosity
you brought the world into being
and gave it life.
Then you gave yourself,
on the cross of human suffering.
Such priceless, painful giving!
Did you invite us here to show us that?
Then show it to us once more, O God!
Show us a different kind of world,
a different cost of living,
where the pain will not be eased
by the money we spend on ourselves
but by the way we spend ourselves for others,
and the way we value life.
Eternal God,
out of your great generosity,
make us generous; bring us into being.
Amen

Brian Woodcock

YOUTH CONCERN

A litany of intercession

A sound is heard in Ramah
the sound of bitter weeping.
Rachel is crying for her children …

A sound is heard in Gaza, the sound of bitter weeping
Pray for the holy innocents of the camps,
   victims of displacement and injustice
LORD HAVE MERCY UPON US, CHRIST HAVE MERCY UPON US

A sound is heard in Malawi, the sound of bitter weeping
Pray for the holy innocents of Southern Africa,
   victims of drought and the IMF
LORD HAVE MERCY UPON US, CHRIST HAVE MERCY UPON US

A sound is heard in Belfast, the sound of bitter weeping
Pray for the holy innocents of Northern Ireland,
   victims of history and self-righteousness
LORD HAVE MERCY UPON US, CHRIST HAVE MERCY UPON US

A sound is heard in London, the sound of bitter weeping
Pray for the holy innocents of Britain,
   victims of indifference and greed
LORD HAVE MERCY UPON US, CHRIST HAVE MERCY UPON US

A sound is heard in Rio, the sound of bitter weeping
Pray for the holy innocents of Brazil,
   victims of cruelty and complicity
LORD HAVE MERCY UPON US, CHRIST HAVE MERCY UPON US

A sound is heard in Los Angeles, the sound of bitter weeping
Pray for the holy innocents of North America,
   victims of prejudice and market forces
LORD HAVE MERCY UPON US, CHRIST HAVE MERCY UPON US

A sound is heard in Bangkok, the sound of bitter weeping
Pray for the holy innocents of Thailand,
   victims of lust and poverty
LORD HAVE MERCY UPON US, CHRIST HAVE MERCY UPON US

A sound is heard in Mindanao, the sound of bitter weeping
Pray for the holy innocents of the Philippines,
   victims of poverty and ethnic strife
LORD HAVE MERCY UPON US, CHRIST HAVE MERCY UPON US

A sound is heard in Bougainville, the sound of bitter weeping
Pray for the holy innocents of the Pacific,
   victims of expendability and profit
LORD HAVE MERCY UPON US, CHRIST HAVE MERCY UPON US

A sound is heard in our town, the sound of bitter weeping
Pray for the holy innocents in our midst,
   victims of violence and selfishness
LORD HAVE MERCY UPON US, CHRIST HAVE MERCY UPON US

Kathy Galloway

Month 3 Day 3

THE WORD

Which word didn't you understand?

Someone once said they were not worried by the parts of the Bible they did not understand. What did bother them was the parts they did understand, and so it is with me. I am not worried by the parts of the Bible I have forgotten or never read, and I am not much bothered by the parts of the Bible and Christian teaching I cannot understand. What disturbs me are the parts that are so clear that it is not possible to misunderstand them, such as the Beatitudes and some other parts of the Sermon on the Mount, or the story of the sheep and the goats where Jesus says exactly what will happen to nations who allow the peoples of other nations to starve, for the only way to avoid the challenge of such passages is to pretend that Jesus meant something else or that, for some reason, what he says does not apply to us.

Roger Gray

HOSPITALITY AND WELCOME

Encounter

1 Kings 17: 8-16

Here is a man
on a journey –
needing somewhere to lay his head,
thirsty, hungry.

Here is a woman
on her home ground –
picking up sticks
wary of strangers.

Both of them are living in a dry land
where a little water, a handful of meal
need to go a long way.

One has a household to feed,
the other has only himself to keep going
through the wilderness,
until God lets him know why.
He is travelling in faith,
she has given up hope.

A coping woman
she has now come to the end
of her resources –

just this last ration of meal,
just this trickle of oil –
not much more water,
sticks for the last fire –
just these embers of courage –
she is burnt out.

He is not sure why he is here,
except that God pointed him this way –
to take the food out of the mouths
of this hungry family?
To walk away? Or to watch them die?
What can he do that will change anything?

But she offers him welcome
and he offers encouragement –
and they go on from there …

Jan Sutch Pickard

THIS IS THE DAY

His body now

It's comparatively easy to believe that God created the world long ago. And it's reasonable to believe that, if that is so, he will do something with the world in the end. It's easy to believe in God in the past and in the future – of our own lives as of the world. It's a terrifying thought to believe in God in the present. And yet the only tense for God is the present tense. He is Lord of the future and the past because he is the great 'I am'.

All of life's problems arise when we say that we believe in God now, when we say he is concerned with all life's happenings now as in the past or in the future. For it means he is concerned with particular events and particular people – all events and all people. The great abstractions lose meaning. God is not Beauty, Truth and Goodness. He is not the Great Impartial. He is known in his actions. And actions cannot be impartial. To believe in God now is to believe in his actions now, with men and in events.

It is this belief in God the Creator, in whose image man is made, and who is ever at work in history, that is the basis of the faith of the Bible; of the New Testament as of the Old; of the New Testament more vividly than of the Old, because more personally.

It is because of this belief that men, some men, were ready to believe in Jesus … The love of God and his purpose in history were shown to them in One who had called them by name and admitted them, through the power of his love, into the fellowship of this new society.

They were his body now, to express his love for men and to be the human instrument of his purposes.

Ralph Morton, 1951

THE IONA EXPERIENCE

Communities of resistance

Geese in a flock have seventy per cent greater range than a single goose on its own; geese in formation fly seventy-five per cent faster than single geese.

Iona, down through the centuries, speaks to us above all about the experience of the Holy Spirit in *community*. The islanders who have always had to be dependent on each other, the Celtic monks, the Benedictines and the present-day Iona Community have all learned about the need and strength of sharing.

Christianity is a community faith. The scriptures of the Old and New Testaments are products of a faith community and can only be understood as such. When Jesus began his ministry, he immediately gathered disciples around him. Right from the beginning, conversion meant a call to discipleship within the context of a community of faith. The New Testament is full of the struggles of the early Christian community as it sought to live out the faith which bound it together.

A key New Testament concept is represented by the Greek word *koinonia*, meaning communion or fellowship. Communion, community, communicate – these words of shared derivation speak of a shared experience and are at the heart of the Christian message. The church is intended to be such a community of participation, yet the actual experience of being in church is often one of isolation. The popularity of places such as Taizé, Corrymeela and Iona testifies to the hunger for community.

When guests come to live in Iona Abbey today, they come to share in the daily life of a resident community which worships and works together year in, year out. The Celtic and Benedictine insistence that all of life is sacred is reflected in the life of the contemporary Iona Community. The group resident in the Abbey all year round tries to work out ways of living together in which resources are shared, people are valued and listened to, and love and trust can be evidenced, despite differences.

Sitting around a refectory table in any one week may be a professor of theology, a Roman Catholic monk, an unemployed teenager, a Quaker peace activist, an army chaplain, a single parent with children, a businessman, a battered wife, an inner-city gang boy and a Presbyterian minister. Many guests have had that experience common to all too many people in today's world – that of being buffeted, rejected and hurt so that they become closed and defensive. The Abbey community aims to be a group where people can feel safe – a sanctuary where they can open out, share their fears, reflect on their lives, share worship and work, and join in discussions on the theme for the week, in which contemporary issues are looked at in the light of the Gospel.

Community life – the life of the people who form each particular week's Abbey community – grows fast as people wash dishes together, worship, engage in arts or music, and chat – at the dinner table, in the common room or chapter house, on walks and out on the weekly pilgrimage round the island. During the course of the week people can expect to be affirmed – and challenged. The mix of age, colour, gender, background and religious affiliation expresses each week an amazing diversity of Christian community.

It would be easy – and wrong – to romanticise Christian community, especially in a location such as Iona. The tensions of living together are not magically dispersed; indeed, they may be increased because of the heightened expectations. The testimony of so many on Iona is that healing comes through living the questions and not accepting easy answers. Somehow, the Church at large must work at ways of restoring real community to its heart, and intentional communities such as Iona can offer hard-won experience in the quest for such an essential recovery. People are not attracted to communities such as Iona simply because of a need for community. It is a particular style of community which is important.

Ron Ferguson

Prayer

Thank you for our time in community
for deep, if fleeting, friendships
for those conversations late at night
for the vulnerable intensity lubricated by laughter
for the freedom to serve others
and to affirm ourselves
in the face of all that you know and we know of our lives
and we thank you for any sign that the churches
with which so many are disaffected
can yet be your body on earth in the community of creation

David Coleman

LIFE IN COMMUNITY

Two women

To Tina and Catherine – with love

They stood together
embracing one another
in the quiet Abbey
on the beautiful island.
Two women –
one with a growing brain tumour,
the other with progressive
neurological disease.
There, in their brokenness
they embraced
And in their joined hands
they held, in love,
the broken bread –
the body of Christ.
And I, in my health,
– stood alone.

They stood together
embracing one another –
on a noisy hill
outside a city.
Two women –
one the broken-hearted mother
the other the anguished friend.

There, in their brokenness
they embraced
And into their empty hands
they received, in love
the broken body of Christ.
And I, with my full hands,
– stood alone.

Frances Hawkey

Women

My dirty womb

Recently, I had the salutary experience of being in church where a version of the 'Liturgy of St James' was sung which included the phrase 'Mary's spotless womb'. I lost the hymn after that – I was too busy thinking through the implications of the phrase. If Mary's womb was spotless, did that mean that mine was spotted, stained, dirty even? And was it dirty because of what had come out of it, or what had been introduced into it? Were the children that had come out of it dirty, or the penis that had gone into it? Were the sexual acts that had resulted in the birth of the children dirty, or the giving birth to them out of it? And what about the sexual acts that hadn't resulted in pregnancy? Were they dirty? Or perhaps it was my very womb itself that was intrinsically dirty, because I had come from one like it? And what did 'dirty' mean, in this context? Did it simply mean dusty or earthy as one's hands might be after gardening, or was it a word loaded with metaphorical content of corruption and decay?

I asked these questions, and I thought of my beautiful children. I thought of the considerable pleasure and occasional moments of ecstasy I have received, and I hope given, in making love. I thought of my forty-four-year-old body, bearing the marks of time, childbirth and breastfeeding, years of carrying shopping, of occasional illness or injury – the marks of mortality. As this body, I have worked, fed people, comforted children and adults, experienced the beauty and tragedy of the world, sung, danced, wept, felt anger and tenderness, experienced pain and weakness, got around more reliably than with any form of mechanised transport … the list is endless.

I was so angry, I nearly walked out of the service. Here is the legacy of the church, still subtly underpinning so much of our understanding of sexuality. Why are we still singing this pernicious garbage? It is not our *bodies* that are in need of redemption, it is our *consciousness*.

I love my body. I love the fact that I am a carnal, sexual being. I am thankful to God with every breath I take for my incarnation, and for the incarnation of Jesus that said a great 'yes' to mine. I hate the things that damage people's bodies (and, indeed, the bodies of animals, and of the earth itself) as much as I hate the things that damage the human spirit, because they cannot be divided. We are unitary beings, whole people. It is a false consciousness that has made one part of our human experience bad and one part good. This is the Christian legacy that we are only now beginning to shake off.

Because I do not feel my body, or anyone else's, for that matter, to be bad, and because dirt for me is a neutral word, to do with dishes or houses that need washed (and, indeed, is sometimes a good word with associations of sweat after energetic activity or earth in a garden) the religious language of purity and impurity to describe sin is meaningless for me. Taboos around menstruation and childbirth, around bodily fluids and natural functions, which may have had their origins in ancient hygiene precautions but were extrapolated into cultural attitudes and practices, especially with regard to women, are not part of my consciousness. That this language still exerts a powerful emotional influence is, for me, an indication that this is a part of the legacy we need to work hard at shaking off. There are many ways to describe the reality of sin – it may be separation, alienation, wrong relationship – but the language of impurity has blighted too many lives already.

Kathy Galloway

A labour of love

This story of creation was written during a Women's Week at Iona Abbey. It offers a woman's reflection on the biblical narrative, highlighting aspects of God's work which are often forgotten. It may be read by one or more people accompanied by suitable music and with abstract slides shown on a central screen.

Once upon a time,
in the beginning,
a labour of love was undertaken.

It started with a sign,
to show that something was about to happen.
Light came forth from the deep darkness,
bright, clear and unmistakable.

And it was very good.

At the second time,
the waters were broken.
At first, they gushed,
then they dried to a trickle,
and a space was created.
It was exactly the right size.
By now, creation was well under way.

And it was very good.

At the third time,
a cradle was made ready.
It was comfortable and beautiful and waiting.
And food was prepared,
issuing warmly and sweetly
and in precisely the right measure
from the being of the labourer.

And it was very good.

At the fourth time,
rhythm was established.
Ebbing and flowing, contracting and expanding,
pain and joy, sun and moon,
beginning and ending.
The labour of love progressed.

And it was very good.

At the fifth time,
there was ceaseless activity:
fluttering like the wings of the dove,
humming like the murmur of the dragonfly,
swimming like the darting golden fish,
wriggling like the lithe serpent,
surging like a mighty lion.

And it was very good.

At the sixth time,
there was a momentary, endless hesitation.
Then a child was born.
And the child looked just like the one who had given it life.
The child, too, was born with the power to create,
and to make decisions,
and to love.

The labourer looked at all that had been accomplished,
and rejoiced,
for it was very good.

At the seventh time,
the labour was finished.

The task was complete,
and the labourer rested,
for she was very, very tired.

Kathy Galloway

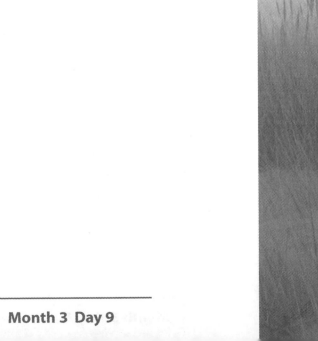

Month 3 Day 9

PRAYER

Silence

When the world tells us
we are what we do with our activity,
acumen or achievement
let us learn
WE ARE WHAT WE DO WITH OUR SILENCE

When the world tells us
we are what we do with our spending power,
selling power, or our power of speech
let us learn
WE ARE WHAT WE DO WITH OUR SILENCE

When the world tells us
to drown the silent sufferings of others
with indifference or noise
or to forget the art of stillness in the storm
let us learn
WE ARE WHAT WE DO WITH OUR SILENCE

When the world tells us
to rush in where angels fear to tread,
let us learn that angels listen first
before they take a step
for the voice of God in the silence …

Giles David

JUSTICE AND PEACE

An informed anger

People who are angry at injustice are compassionate people: they are filled with passion and they do not make docile citizens: angry people (slaves and free people) forced the end of slavery in the British empire; angry people (men and women) won the vote for women; angry people (black and white) brought an end to apartheid in South Africa. Angry people can change the rules … Compassion enlivens and empowers the heart and mind so that with an informed anger we ask questions.

Joy Mead

Inspired by love and anger
(Tune: Salley Gardens, Irish folk tune)

Inspired by love and anger,
disturbed by need and pain,
informed of God's own bias,
we ask him once again:
'How long must some folk suffer?
How long can few folk mind?
How long dare vain self-interest
turn prayer and pity blind?'

From those forever victims
of heartless human greed,
their cruel plight composes
a litany of need:
'Where are the fruits of justice?
Where are the signs of peace?
When is the day when prisoners
and dreams find their release?'

From those forever shackled
to what their wealth can buy,
the fear of lost advantage
provokes the bitter cry,
'Don't query our position!
Don't criticise our wealth!
Don't mention those exploited
by politics and stealth!'

Month 3 Day 11

To God, who through the prophets
proclaimed a different age,
we offer earth's indifference,
its agony and rage:
'When will the wronged be righted
When will the kingdom come?
When will the world be generous
to all instead of some?'

God asks, 'Who will go with me?
Who will extend my reach?
And who, when few will listen,
will prophesy and preach?
And who, when few bid welcome,
will offer all they know?
And who, when few dare follow,
will walk the road I show?'

Amused in someone's kitchen,
asleep in someone's boat,
attuned to what the ancients
exposed, proclaimed and wrote,
a saviour without safety,
a tradesman without tools
has come to tip the balance
with fishermen and fools.

John L Bell and Graham Maule

THE INTEGRITY OF CREATION

Every time we see a rainbow

In the story of the flood we read that Noah was a good man, a man of integrity who had found favour with God. But for the rest of creation – humans, animals, reptiles and birds – God said, 'I regret having made them.' In the eyes of God, 'the wickedness of man was great on earth ... the earth grew corrupt ... and filled with violence' (Genesis 6).

When God looks on his creation today, some thousands of years after Noah, does he not see a situation similar to the pre-ark days of Noah? Wickedness? Corruption? Violence? Greed? Self-interest? Very few are taking the threat to creation seriously. Lots of words, lots of promises, but always lots of reasons why 'Not us' or 'Not us yet' or 'Not us until everyone else does'.

Climate change is a fact. The forecast of the amount and rate of change and consequent effects may differ between agencies and researchers but the reason for change is not in dispute. The concentration of carbon dioxide, one of the so-called 'greenhouse' gases, in the atmosphere is now greater than at any time during any interglacial period in the history of the planet earth over the last forty million years. According to a recent (2000) report of the Royal Commission on Environmental Pollution[1], 'there is no precedent in recent geological history to help us understand precisely what consequences will follow ... the speed at which carbon dioxide concentration is changing appears to be unparalleled in geological history.'

But the more alarming and plausible forecasts of the consequences of global warming are that we are fast approaching a 'positive feedback' situation (meaning that one consequence triggers another action which reinforces the first.

Unchecked, it leads to a disastrous, catastrophic end.) One example of such an effect, quoted by Aubrey Meyer in a Schumacher briefing[2] is the release of massive quantities of methane, a much more powerful greenhouse gas than carbon dioxide, from hydrate in the Arctic seabed and from permafrost, which at present covers about a third of the planet, following an initial slight warming of Arctic regions. The first small release would lead to warming and thus an increased release of methane which would result in a thermal runaway – goodbye life on earth!

Today it is not God who is destroying life on earth but humans who have failed in the stewardship task entrusted to them by God. The industrialised nations are the worst offenders. Twenty per cent of the world's population (the so called 'developed' world) are responsible for 80% of greenhouse gas emissions and receive 80% of the world's income. There is, not surprisingly, a very strong correlation between emissions and GNP. Former US President George Bush the elder refused to sign the 1991 United Nations Framework Convention on Climate Change because of the economic growth interests of the USA until it had been so watered down as to be ineffective. George Bush the younger withdrew the USA from the Kyoto Protocol. Meanwhile gas concentrations continue to rise to disaster levels.

We can expect more and more 'unnatural' disasters worldwide. Already in the UK some properties are becoming uninsurable because of flood risk. It has been assessed that if storm damage continues to grow at its present rate (about 10% a year) by 2050 the annual damage to property resulting from climate change will exceed the total value of everything that humanity will produce in that year. Neither insurance companies nor governments will be able to underwrite the losses. Is God again regretting creation?

Every time we see a rainbow let us ask ourselves: are we respecting our side of God's covenant with his people?

John Harrison

COLUMBAN CHRISTIANITY & THE CELTIC TRADITION

Walking together

A fruitful way to celebrate Columba's life could be to rethink the meaning of mission in the light of its meaning to those in the Celtic tradition.

The very word is being put out of currency today as an acceptable word in South America. Down the centuries, especially since the time of the Spanish Conquistadors, it has stood for the imposition of an imperial European version of the Christian faith on a defeated people, by fire and sword made subject to their conquerors. In more recent times, there still lingers in the flavour of the word a sense of the enlightened instructing the unenlightened in a one-way traffic. In this century we have become more aware of these distortions. To combat them, South Americans speak rather of 'walking together'. The phrase suggests mutuality and solidarity rather than a relationship of spiritual superiors and inferiors. It brings to mind Amos's question (3:3), 'Can two walk together except they be agreed?'

The sending of Abraham out of his own land was a kind of motto for the Celtic mission. The Latin American understanding of 'walking together' with Christ, with other Christians, with enquirers, with pagans, is close to their emphasis on pilgrimage.

Ian M Fraser

Racism

We have a choice

Racism is a sin. Of course, this is nothing new. It was true from the beginning for the followers of Jesus. Those who saw how he identified with the marginalised and witnessed his compassion for and solidarity with people of other races, cultures and faiths knew that racism was wrong. Pentecost was the denial of racial division and narrow nationalism. The encounter between Peter, a Jew, and Cornelius, the Roman Centurion, tells us that with God there is no superior race. In Antioch we find the followers of Jesus already living as a multiracial, multi-cultural group – Jews, Cypriots, Greeks, Cyrenians and at least one black man.

So what went wrong? Sadly, the temptations of power, influence, privilege and domination were to prove too attractive over against the very different dynamic of humility, compassion and service to others offered to us by Jesus.

In Britain, racism is a denial of our democratic tradition. But for Christians racism denies the unity and solidarity of all humanity which is at the heart of the gospel. We have a choice. To do nothing, or to take up the challenge.

Stanley Hope

The monster

For over thirty years a monster has been loose in Britain
It was born out of political weakness
It has grown into a dangerous source of political power
It is a frightening creature, cruel and inhuman
It has many arms, appendages, feelers, agents
Its influence touches most areas of our national life
It finds a home in many of our national institutions
It has little respect for compassion, justice or common sense
Its victims are the weak, the vulnerable, the unwanted
It undermines our democracy and the integrity of Britain
It has to be confronted and destroyed.

For those killed by the monster
For those refused entry to their country of citizenship
For the Asian women subjected to virginity testing
For those unjustly removed or deported
For those detained without trial
For all separated families
For those denied visits to relatives in Britain
For our treatment of asylum seekers
For all who have been ignored,
humiliated, degraded by the system
For the loss of our own humanity

We express our shame and ask forgiveness
We commit ourselves to work for a fair and just immigration policy.

Stanley Hope

Month 3 Day 14

COMMUNITY

Can 'community' return?

The last hundred years, in Western communities, have seen the individual becoming lonelier and more isolated from others. Friends in Africa and India are amazed when they learn that, in our country, folk can die in their homes and not be found for several weeks. Dead behind their own front door, but without anyone knowing. They find it impossible to believe that not one single other person would call at their house over the course of a few weeks. And they contrast that kind of isolation with the endless comings and goings in their own homes. It is still true that in many parts of the world it takes a whole village to raise a child.

Having said this, I also believe that our Western societies are now searching, at a whole variety of levels, for the restoration of 'community' – a word heard these days from government officials. It has become a buzz word; a warm word: community policing, community care, community studies, youth and community work, community churches. George Hillery listed ninety-four uses of the term, the only feature they had in common being a concern about people. Despite this wide usage, the basic question remains: can 'community' in the sense of people being mutually accountable to one another ever return in a society which prizes so highly the individual and personal self-enhancement?

Peter Millar

East 53rd Street, Chicago

Who are you, my neighbour,
on this crowded street?
We live close by
in our tiny apartments
and share the changing seasons.
But do we know each other
not as strangers, but as friends?
Your family is far away, like mine;
yours in El Salvador, mine in Scotland –
two different worlds.
You came as a refugee, I through choice
and now we're on the same street
alone, in our tiny apartments
separated only by a wall.
And around us a vast city
glittering, yet vulnerable,
where so many like us
have found food and shelter
but not always freedom from fear.

Month 3 Day 15

Let's meet and talk one day
and share our stories,
and maybe our tears.
For the lights on our street
are Christmas lights –
reminding us of another Story
where strangers meet
and find each other.
It's the story of Jesus,
the One who is always here
on East 53rd Street
in south Chicago

Peter Millar

PILGRIMAGE

A counter-cultural journey

The reawakening to mystery is leading us to an acceptance of the provisional. Of understanding life as, essentially, a pilgrimage. An exploration rather than an arrival. And here on the island of Iona on the west coast of Scotland we are often moved and touched by our Celtic inheritance, which itself opens up new truths in this particular area of provisionality.

The Celtic peoples lived against the struggles of nature and the natural order. Life was uncertain – as it still is in many cultures today. There was this deep acceptance that the provisional was at the heart of human experience. And we see that again replicated in so many stories of the gospel writers. For those living in late modernity this, in itself, is a counter-cultural journey. Particularly in society where security, not only financial security, but security at all levels, has become a primary motivating factor. And yet, as we read the gospels, and as the gospel stories announce themselves to us, the ability, in Christ, to take risks, to be on a pilgrimage, to seek, is in fact at the heart of many of these realities.

Peter Millar

The walk of faith

But pilgrimage is also a sign of contradiction, and of resistance to our prevailing value system, that of the market. Pilgrimage, after all, has no function other than itself; its means is as important as its end, its process as its product. Its utility value is small, and its benefits cannot be quantified or costed. Its value is intrinsic. It is something that is good to do because it is good to do. It states clearly that the extravagant gesture (because it is extravagant in terms of time and commitment) is an irrepressible part of what it means to be human and to walk on the earth. And whether the context for pilgrimage is solitude or community, we will be drawn deeper into the mystery of God and the care of creation.

Kathy Galloway

Bless to us, O God,
the earth beneath our feet.
Bless to us, O God,
the path whereon we go.
Bless to us, O God,
the people whom we meet.
Amen.

SEXUALITY

Why should this be so difficult?

Last year I played at a ceilidh attended by almost 400 folk which was part of the increasingly successful Lesbian, Gay, Bisexual and Transgender Arts Festival, Glasgay. The band unanimously agree that these are among the best gigs we have. There is something incredibly unique and wonderful about so many people having the opportunity (if they wish) to dance with the same sex! Yet why should this be so unusual?

As a result of these gigs, three couples have approached us at different times to ask if we will play for the evening receptions following their 'same sex blessings'. Two of the couples have still to set a date for their 'big day' (one wishes to wait until gay marriage becomes legal!). One lesbian couple, however, hope to have their 'special day' in April of this year. They wish, like many straight couples, to publicly profess their love for and commitment to each other within a Christian setting and have been trying to find a minister to help them plan and conduct their ceremony. Needless to say, they haven't found this an easy task. Yet why should this be so difficult?

The success of Glasgay is only one of many indicators that gay, lesbian and bisexual people are increasingly being accepted within mainstream society. Unfortunately the institutional church is seriously lagging behind. Those in positions of power seem determined to maintain the view that heterosexual marriage is the only acceptable norm – and if you're not straight and married, you're either morally suspect or a social misfit. Why is this not being challenged more strongly? Part of the reason, I believe, is a 'culture of fear' which prevents the Church from seriously grappling with the issue of sexuality. In consequence, many Christian men and women continue to experience a sense of alienation from the faith community to which they wish to belong.

Neil Squires

HEALING

Renaming ourselves

This renaming, so beloved of God, is a holy ministry to which the Church and its members are called. For all of us have a 'past' and all of us have problems, and all of us can live under the cloud of who or what we have been, and what is up with us now.

One of the less savoury aspects of contemporary society seems to be the desire to categorise people according to their deficiencies, rather than call them by their names.

So we talk about the physically challenged, the mentally challenged, the abuse victim, the anorexic, the overeater, the divorcee, the single parent, the cross-dresser, the agoraphobic.

And true as these descriptions might be, there are two greater truths with which we have to deal in the face of Jesus Christ.

The one is that God does not define us by our problems or our past. And if God does not, why should we?

There is a phrase which has crept into common currency in many churches, a good phrase as originally used by a Roman Catholic theologian. It is the phrase *wounded healer*. It echoes the thought of Dietrich Bonhoeffer that *'only a suffering God can help'*. In order to be the means of restoration, Christ makes himself vulnerable, wounded, at one with humanity, and out of pain and rejection completes the work of salvation.

Applied to Christians, it can suggest that those best able to help others are people who are aware of their own weaknesses.

I would fully endorse the efficacy of this kind of solidarity as a means to recovery. But sometimes those who see themselves as wounded healers spend more time talking about their wounds and encouraging voyeurism than enabling the healing process to begin.

God does not define us by our problems or our past. Nor should we. There are times when Jane, the overweight single mother, has to leave the baggage behind and be plain Jane. There are times when Robert, the abused ex-con, has to let his past be past and simply be Robert.

The bent-double woman whom Jesus healed would never have been completely cured as long as she was diminished by the stigma which had been attached to her. She had both to walk tall and to believe that her prime identity was that of a daughter of Abraham, a beautiful child of God.

Are you prepared to walk as one whose main description is a beautiful child of God – or are you going to hang on to the other names you call yourself or others call you?

God does not define us by our problems.

John L. Bell

SOCIAL ACTION

'Give me a drink'

Jesus Christ never asked those who met him to become a rabbi like himself. He always asked them to do what they could for him, even when it was a simple request like, 'Give me a drink.'

For it is when we use the potentials God has given us to advance the purposes of his kingdom that we become partners with, rather than strangers to, our Lord.

I do not know you. I do not know your potentials. I do not know what for you would be the equivalent of Jesus Christ asking the woman at the well for a drink.

But I do know that when you give to God and do for God whatever you can, you move from the fringe to the centre, from isolation to belonging, from doubt to understanding, from conversation to conversion.

John L. Bell

CHURCH RENEWAL

Loitering with intent

I have a friend (I don't have many) who went to a school run by a church. He describes the experience as 'Colditz meets the weakest link'. And he couldn't get out fast enough. Sadly this has meant that organised religion is a no-go area for him. Even attending rites of passage in churches today brings him out in a cold sweat.

However, that does not mean my friend is not religious. In fact, he is one of the most spiritual people I have ever known. He translates that spirituality into working for a church-based, community-based organisation that helps the poor, the sick, the struggling and the rejected, of whom there are many, take control of their lives. In fact, he manages the project, and does so brilliantly. Many people have had their lives changed by my friend's work. What matters to the project, and the church whose ministry it is, is that the work is done to the highest possible standard, not whether someone goes to church once in a blue moon.

But, according to the rules of some churches and Christian organisations involved in the same kind of work, my friend would not be eligible to work for them in any way, shape or form. This is because he is, and I quote from one of those churches, 'a pagan'. (In other words, he has no live church connection.) According to these Christians, this deeply spiritual individual, who gives his life to serving others, would 'undermine the ethos' of their work. If, however, my friend were a member of a church, irrespective of how often he attended, what his theology was, how racist, homophobic, anti-women he was, etc. etc., he would be seen to add something special to their 'ethos' …

Jesus did not discriminate. He loitered with those discriminated against by others. He called people to change their way of life but he never suggested that only those who followed him could speak of God. In his parable he never said that the Good Samaritan needed to change his religion to be a good neighbour, or that the forgiving father had to attend the temple to welcome back his prodigal son.

Jesus loitered more with those who were not religious than with those who were. Jesus's example was not to build a holier-than-thou enclave but to loiter in the places the powerful were too scared to go. We are called to loiter with those who would not expect us ever to be beside them, to be in the places the Church is not associated with, amongst the excluded and rejected, the struggling and suffering. If we then, in our structure and policies, exclude those folk from being part of our work, then we fail to loiter. We simply patronise and reject again.

Ewan Aitken

WORSHIP

As much an offering to God as anything done in church

The great gift that I feel I have received from the Iona Community – from God – is the expression, in the Community's life, of the central Christian insight into the integrity of worship. We have long put this into words by using the phrase about 'work and worship'. But it's more than that. For me the excitement of Iona, when I first came, was discovering that not only was 'worship' not simply what religious people did in church, but that worship was everything that Christian disciples did and offered to God, and that this could be expressed in a style of living open and accessible to anyone, anywhere.

On Iona, in the building days, this insight was of course expressed in the context appropriate to that stage in the life of the Community. Thus, each day, men came to the morning service in their working clothes – and consciously saw their work on the walls as their daily worship. Minister-members each day both shared in the work on the walls and took part in what was called 'ministers' craftsmanship' – lectures, discussions, sermon preparation, etc. All this was 'worth-ship': services were part of that, and needed to be prepared and led well – but they were only *part* of worship, never the whole thing.

In expressing the integrity of worship in this way, at that time, the Community was making some significant statements. It was saying something significant, for instance, about what church worship should be about: about God, certainly, but about God Incarnate, and about God's world, this world. But it was also saying something significant about daily life – that all life is sacred, and that the living of it, and the work done in it, was as much an offering to God as anything done in church.

John Harvey

WORK

The power of ceremony

George MacLeod, the founder of the Iona Community, said, 'Only a demanding common task builds community.' The Iona Community was founded to be a sign of the rebuilding of the common life, the reintegration of the sacred and the secular, of prayer and politics, of the material and the spiritual. The common task through which it set about this rebuilding was the restoration of the ruined monastic buildings on the island of Iona. But the ceremony which named this common task took place every morning before the day's labours began.

In the Abbey church, ministers and craftsmen stood to make their responses:

Unless the Lord builds the house
THEY LABOUR IN VAIN THAT BUILD IT.

Unless the Lord keeps the city
THE WATCHMAN WAKETH BUT IN VAIN.

O Lord, do good in Thy good measure
BUILD THOU THE WALLS OF JERUSALEM.

O Lord, make speed to save us
O LORD, MAKE HASTE TO HELP US

Praise ye the Lord
THE LORD'S NAME BE PRAISED

And so, in the words of the 127th Psalm, the Community named the truth that defined the common task. And the Abbey was rebuilt, and the Community was built. Without that ceremony to remind us of that truth, it would not have happened. The two are inseparable.

The building of community is crucial to human existence, for only in community can justice and love be done. Only in community is found responsibility – the activity of responding, the demands of accountability to and for others. This, St Paul tells us, is the nature of the church – to be the Body, wherein no part acts independently of another, and wherein if one part hurts, all are hurt, wherein we are interdependent.

Kathy Galloway

Christ the worker

Leader: Christ the worker

All: Christ the worker,
              born in Bethlehem,
              born to work and die
              for everyone.

Leader: Blessed man-child,

All: Blessed man-child,
              boy of Nazareth,
              grew in wisdom as
              He grew in skill.

Leader: Skilful craftsman

All: Skilful craftsman,
              blessed carpenter,
              praising God by labour
              at his bench,

Leader: Yoke-maker

All: Yoke-maker,
          fashioned by His hands,
          easy yokes that made
          the labour less.

Leader: All who labour

All: All who labour,
          listen to his call,
          He will make that heavy
          burden light.

Leader: Heavy laden,

All: Heavy laden,
          gladly come to Him,
          He will ease your load
          and give you rest.

Leader: Christ the worker

All: Christ the worker,
          love alive for us,
          teach us how to do
          all work for God.

Tom Colvin

CALLED TO BE ONE

'Open to all'

I visited a handsome church in Italy one holiday morning. Over its west door was written: 'Non patet impiis.' Maybe it sounds less offensive in Latin, but in Scots these words mean, 'It's no' for the likes o' us.'

The Law Society of Scotland has as its motto the slogan 'Nihil humanum alienum puto' – 'If it's human, it's our business.' Edinburgh's Royal Infirmary puts it even more succinctly: 'Open to all.' The Church has a lesson to learn from these secular institutions.

Maxwell Craig

MISSION

Moratorium on mission

The plea, in some cases, for a moratorium – a break in the flow of money, personnel, etc., from richer parts of the world to poorer parts – may not represent hostile action but action for survival and identity. Where the mere presence of Europeans produces impotence, then their best service may be to get right out and to offer those they have sought to serve time and breathing space to develop their own particular form of Christian life. If this brings a time of helpless suffering, of breakdown, that may be the gift that those who have been only too dominating owe to the dominated.

This is what was experienced by the Sabaneto Community in the north of the Dominican Republic. They numbered about ten. In an area where the struggle was to rise to subsistence level, they had to live hand to mouth, with, at best, irregular employment. Yet they were Christians who were alert to their situation and had become convinced that they should not be the victims but rather agents of change in it, in the hope that the whole area might become one of greater justice and opportunity for poor campesinos.

This awakening of a new hope had been stimulated and encouraged by the contribution of people from other lands. But the day came when they believed they had to part from their last expatriate worker and, with him, from the skills he brought and the finance which can always be tapped when someone comes from a richer land. Some time later I put this question to them: 'Would you like to have the help of expatriate staff again?'

They thought a while. Outside help had obviously done a great deal for them. Then, one by one, they gave the same answer: 'No. It has been a painful experience, it has been a bit like a death. We have often not known how to carry on. But we now begin to see, at last, that there cannot be resurrection without this death; and we are becoming resurrected as a community who make their own decisions, even though what we do seems so inadequate in the face of the needs of this whole area.'

Missionary, go home ... or stay

A statement on the future of mission originating in the traditional sending areas was made by Bishop F. Pagura to the Missionary Liaison committee of Costa Rica, where he served until the early 1970s:

- *If you cannot understand what is happening in this continent, in this hour in which it awakens to the dawn of a new liberation: Missionary, go home.*

- *If you are not able to separate the eternal word of the gospel from the cultural moulds in which you brought it to those lands and even taught it with true abnegation: Missionary, go home.*

- *If you cannot identify with the sufferings, anguish and aspirations of these peoples made prematurely old by an unequal struggle that would seem not to have end or hope: Missionary, go home.*

- *If your alliance and fidelity to the nation of your origin is stronger than your loyalty and obedience to Jesus Christ who has come to 'put down the mighty from their thrones and exalt those of low degree' (Luke 1:52): Missionary, go home.*

- *If your dogmatism is such that it does not permit you to revise your theology and ideology in the light of all the biblical testimony and the happenings of these times: Missionary, go home.*

- *If you are not able to love and respect as equals those whom one day you came to evangelise as 'lost': Missionary, go home.*

- *If you cannot rejoice with the entrance of new peoples and churches into a new period of maturity, of independence, of responsibility, even at the price of committing errors such as those you and your countrymen committed also in the past, then it is time to return home.*

  But if you are willing to share the risks and pains of this hour of birth which our American peoples are living, even denying yourself;

- *if you begin to rejoice with them because of the joy of feeling that the gospel is not only announcement and affirmation of a remote hope, but of a hope and a liberation that is already transforming history;*

- *if you are willing to put more of your time, of your values, of your life at the service of these people who are awakening,*

  then stay, since there is much to be done, and hands and blood are needed for such an immense enterprise in which Christ is pioneer and protagonist.

Ian M Fraser

THE POOR AND DISADVANTAGED

The meaning of the Eucharist

(Here interviewed in a 'safe house' in the Philippines while being hunted by the police, Ed De La Torre – a Filipino theologian/politician/activist was the guest of the Iona Community at its Community Week, 1991.)

'One Christmas, a group of about a hundred farmers came up here to demand land from the government. We held a midnight mass. We were reflecting on what that meant and I felt that one of them expressed it well when he said, "The Christian meaning of what we are doing is this, no? At the Eucharist we have only a few hosts, only a little bread, and we break it up and give it to each other. Why is this? It is really an act of the poor. There is not enough, that's why we break it up. If there were enough for all we would all get a whole piece."

'Another farmer's observation is even more profound: "Even if there is not enough, we will not follow the logic of the development economists who say, 'Let's first increase the GNP. Then, if there is not enough, we will make sure that we first feed those who are strong enough to work. Others can take their chance.' No! we won't postpone the sharing. There will not be enough for everyone but no one will have nothing."

'The whole point is not abundance or scarcity but that we share in a real celebration. We are not just going to glorify scarcity for scarcity's sake as more heroic. Even more importantly, we are to share what there is available in the period of poverty. What is most important is our solidarity.

'There was no explicit reference in this to the Last Supper but I think the farmer, in his own way, was articulating a very profound Eucharist, which I personally could not achieve with all my priestly training.'

Ian M Fraser

Among the poor
Advent litany

A: Among the poor,
B: among the proud,
A: among the persecuted,
B: among the privileged,
A: Christ is coming,
ALL: HE IS COMING TO MAKE ALL THINGS NEW.

A: In the private house,
B: in the market place,
A: in the wedding feast,
B: in the judgement hall,
A: Christ is coming,
ALL: HE IS COMING TO MAKE ALL THINGS NEW.

A: With a gentle touch,
B: with an angry word,
A: with a clear conscience,
B: with burning love,
A: Christ is coming,
ALL: HE IS COMING TO MAKE ALL THINGS NEW.

A: That the kingdom might come,
B: that the world might believe,
A: that the powerful might stumble,
B: that the humble might be raised,
A: Christ is coming,
ALL: HE IS COMING TO MAKE ALL THINGS NEW.

A: Within us,
B: without us,
A: among us,
B: before us,
A: in this place,
B: in every place,
A: for this time,
B: for all time,
A: Christ is coming,
ALL: HE IS COMING TO MAKE ALL THINGS NEW.

John L. Bell

INTERFAITH

Uncle Wes

Bidwill is part of the Mount Druitt area of Western Sydney – a vast multi-cultural area carrying many markers of poverty and powerlessness.

> Bidwill's streets
> mirror its rainbow people;
> not the movers and shakers
> of down-town Sydney
> but the fragile ones
> from many lands;
> those on the edges
> whose stories reflect
> the raw faces
> of urban desolation.
> Like Uncle Wes,
> displaced from his ancestral land
> where his forebears
> have belonged
> for 60,000 years.
> Not one of the powerful,
> but a prophet for our age,
> revealing the contours
> of our human journey
> into the next millennium.
> A story-teller,

whose ancient wisdom
illumines our
fragmented time.
A dreamer, whose visions enlarge
our capacity for wonder
and remind us
of the mystery of Spirit.
Yet can we hear
his quiet words of life
before our restless greed
brings death to planet Earth,
and be transformed
by knowledge
so different from our own?
The choice is ours,
as God made clear
so long ago.

Peter and Dorothy Millar

NONVIOLENCE AND PEACEKEEPING

'Some of the most violent people I have met are pacifists'

Some of the most violent people I have met are pacifists. But often such violence arises out of deeply felt passion, and passion with all of its content of suffering and joy is surely biblical. I don't think the money-changers in the Temple hung about to argue with Jesus. Revisiting Gethsemane must mean revisiting the agonising dilemma of how to face and transform the full horror and ugliness of violence, sin and injustice in our world.

Perhaps we need to probe more deeply into the meanings of words like 'peace' and 'nonviolence'. Peace is one of those words that needs to be reclaimed. For too long it has been narrowed down to the absence of war, a kind of bland, dove-filled harmony. Perhaps the rounded biblical *shalom* is closer: a strong, robust well-being where justice is an integral part without which there can be no peace.

But history has shown time and again that justice won by violent means already sows the deadly seeds of the next conflict. When I worked in Vietnam, my sympathies were almost entirely with the North Vietnamese revolutionary struggle, and it seemed that the quickest way to achieve justice for the suffering Vietnamese was for the North Vietnamese to win the war as quickly as possible. Which is what, ultimately, they did, but, although the immediate prospect of peace was welcome, already a new powerful group was oppressing, killing, torturing, and the cycle of violence and injustice remained unbroken.

Of course it is easy for me to write – white, privileged, unscathed – and I have often been deeply challenged and moved by people from South Africa, Nicaragua, Chile, Chechnya – the list is endless – who say convincingly, with great authority, that the suffering they experienced left them no other option than reluctantly to pick up a gun. To such people I can only say that I hope I might have the courage to stand with them shoulder to shoulder.

But I still believe that the means of achieving justice must be compatible with the desired end. The tragedy of South Africa is that the bitterness of the structural violence of apartheid has bred a society still trapped in a violent cycle. Bombing the Kosovan Albanians back into power has shattered the birth of civic society and created a counter-flow of Serb refugees with another round of atrocity stories.

This is where, I believe, nonviolence can provide a way forward. I totally agree that 'nonviolence which allows violating to go on is a form of violence itself'[1] – in fact it is not nonviolence. The very essence of nonviolence is that it resists and opposes all forms of injustice and oppression to the last drop of its blood. It can never consent to anything that degrades the human spirit.

Nonviolence is about revolution. It is about finding creative, imaginative ways to overthrow all forms of tyranny and oppression, without becoming the oppressor in the process. It widens the options and holds out a possibility of a way out of the cycle of violence where dignity can be maintained.

A nonviolent response to Kosovo can never be 'Let Kosovo burn.' It calls for intervention. Massive intervention. But intervention with a difference that sends in unarmed observers, bodyguards, mediators, civilian peace teams trained in resistance.

Martin Luther King may ultimately be right in saying: 'The choice is nonviolence or nonexistence.'

Helen Steven

An idea whose time has come

During George MacLeod's funeral a picture came to me of George fixing Jesus with a piercing glare and saying, 'Are you totally committed to nonviolence?'

George passionately believed that nonviolence is 'an idea whose time has come'; with Martin Luther King who said 'nonviolence or nonexistence' ... this passionate commitment took many forms. Organisational ones, being President of the Fellowship of Reconciliation; speaking, preaching, writing on themes of nonviolence; constantly challenging clergy with questions; exploring the diversity of the implications of nonviolence through tax withholding; criticising the violence of the world banking system; making the links between nonviolence and the ecological despoliation of the planet. In so many issues his understanding of the implications of nonviolence took him far ahead of his contemporaries, making his a clear prophetic voice. True, his methods of tackling issues and people were often direct and confrontational – even divisive, but the urgency of 'an idea whose time has come' was driving him onwards and left little room for tact.

Towards the end of his life the nuances and complexities of nonviolence fell away, and George was left with a single-minded passion or obsession which drove him furiously right up to the end. On one occasion he struggled through by taxi from Edinburgh to Glasgow in his determination to see a publication through.

Even in the last days of his life the story goes of him lying on the floor asking Ron Ferguson and Maxwell MacLeod if they were committed to nonviolence. Always that question.

I am left with it burning in my heart.

Helen Steven

BASIC CHRISTIAN COMMUNITIES

A community at worship
'We fight on'

In Oporto, Portugal, the service which mustered the small basic Christian communities in that area for a monthly celebration lasted from 10 am to 5 pm. The first twenty minutes or so were spent in members hugging one another, exchanging greetings, and getting up to date with the news. This was all part of the worship. The first hymn was one composed in the community. It was not only sung but danced. Bible readings followed. Then about an hour's sermon/reflection was built up from these. The small groups had met during the previous week and struggled to see how insights from the text could illuminate their life in the world. There was a mature interpretation.

In the early afternoon we shared a common meal – very much a feature of the worship of basic Christian communities. Mario, the worker-priest then prepared the Eucharist.

All this sounds too good to be true. But are these people 'spiritual athletes'? Anything but. Listen to them when, the bread broken and the wine poured out, they tell of their own brokenness and pour out their hearts in union with the bread and wine. You will hear of frustration and failure in relationships affecting husbands, wives, young people, parents. You will be told of illnesses and despondencies. There will be word of humiliations and stresses at work, in searching for work. 'Cast down, but not destroyed' – the words come instinctively to mind.

The theme for the day is 'How are we to live the joy of our faith?' Sorrows once shared, testimonies are made to a power which overcomes in and through suffering. Isabel, tears streaming down her cheeks from the remembered vexation of being blamed by her employers for taking a week off work to calm a suspected ulcer on doctor's orders, brightens. Her face becomes sun shining through rain. She ends, with quiet firmness, 'We fight on.' (She died of cancer within a year.)

Members of the community do not depart until they have consolidated plans for the political and social engagements to which faith directs them. Some of these they will fulfil together, some separately.

Prayer

Father, Son and Holy Spirit

You are basic community. Your relationship of love and mutual self-giving is the foundation of all true human community. That gives hope.

We give you praise that you are not content with your own society but call us to share in it. We bless and thank you for the love which takes such a risk. May we live in you, that the communities we form may not be based on superficial attraction, but rest on your own mutual delight in self-giving.

Teach us to accept one another as Jesus Christ has accepted us – in our differences, in our awkwardnesses, in our peculiarities – that a building of God may be firmly made out of different-shaped stones. Enable us to accept one another just as we are, not trimmed into smooth conformities.

Lead us to awareness of our uniqueness, of the identity you give us and the destiny you prepare for us. May we all take shape according to what you have in mind for us, and lend this as a strength to others.

Help us, in an age of individualism, to discard opportunity for getting on for ourselves at the expense of others.

Month 3 Day 28

Enable us, in families, to honour each other's particularity and need for space – for you are there; and to show mutual concern and seek to live together in unity of spirit – for you are one.

Bring nations into new community with one another, strengthening the agencies which provide means for international peacemaking.

Since the Church was brought into being to be a sign, instrument and foretaste of the Kingdom of justice, truth and peace which is penetrating the whole fabric of human society, grant that it may look to you for life and be to others a community of love and self-giving.

And to you, Father, Son and Holy Spirit, be glory in the Church and in Christ Jesus throughout the ages.

Amen

Ian M Fraser

Month 3 Day 28

COMMITMENT

Will you come and follow me?
(tune: Kelvingrove, Scottish traditional)

Will you come and follow me
if I but call your name?
Will you go where you don't know
and never be the same?
Will you let my love be shown,
will you let my name be known,
will you let my life be grown
in you and you in me?

Will you leave yourself behind
if I but call your name?
Will you care for cruel and kind
and never be the same?
Will you risk the hostile stare
should your life attract or scare?
Will you let me answer prayer
in you and you in me?

Will you let the blinded see
if I but call your name?
Will you set the prisoners free
and never be the same?
Will you kiss the leper clean
and do such as this unseen,
and admit to what I mean
in you and you in me?

Will you love the 'you' you hide
if I but call your name?
Will you quell the fear inside
and never be the same?
Will you use the faith you've found
to reshape the world around
through my sight and touch and sound
in you and you in me?

Lord, your summons echoes true
when you but call my name.
Let me turn and follow you
and never be the same.
In your company I'll go
where your love and footsteps show.
Thus I'll move and live and grow
in you and you in me.

John L. Bell & Graham Maule

THE REDISCOVERY OF SPIRITUALITY

The incarnation

The Iona Community did not see itself as having a theology of its own. It was not an alternative church: its creeds were those of the national Church of Scotland; it did, however, have particular emphases.

The doctrine most emphasised by the Community was that of the Incarnation – the coming of God to humanity in the shape of Jesus Christ. God, in love, had entered the human situation in all its mess and glory. Humanity had thus been dignified and ennobled. The spiritual had been joined in the material in Jesus Christ, and the material could therefore never be despised. Since the face of Jesus was to be discerned in the poor, the hungry, the prisoners and the victims, social and political action could never be divorced from spirituality.

'The Gospel claims the key to all material issues,' wrote George MacLeod, 'is to be found in the mystery that Christ came in a body: and healed bodies and fed bodies: and that he died bodily and himself rose in his body; to save man body and soul.'

Glory to God in the High Street

In his book, *Only One Way Left*, consisting of the Cunningham lectures delivered in Edinburgh and New York, Dr MacLeod used an illustration which neatly summed up his view of the Incarnation and its implications:

A boy threw a stone at the stained glass window of the Incarnation. It nicked out the 'E' in the word HIGHEST in the text, 'GLORY TO GOD IN THE HIGHEST'. Thus, till unfortunately it was mended, it read, 'GLORY TO GOD IN THE HIGH ST'.

At least the mended E might have been contrived on a swivel so that in a high wind it would have been impossible to see which way it read. Such is the genius, and the offence, of Christian revelation. Holiness, salvation, glory are all come down to earth in Jesus Christ our Lord. Truth is found in the constant interaction of the claim that the apex of the Divine Majesty is declared in Christ's humanity. The Word of God cannot be dissociated from the Action of God. As the blood courses through the body, so the spiritual is alone kept healthy in its interaction in the High Street.

In a stunning and oft-quoted paragraph, the Community's founder talked about the relationship of the action of God to High Streets everywhere:

I simply argue that the Cross be raised again at the centre of the market-place as well as on the steeple of the church. I am recovering the claim that Jesus was not crucified in a cathedral between two candles, but on a cross between two thieves; on the town garbage-heap; at a crossroad so cosmo-politan that they had to write his title in Hebrew and in Latin and in Greek (or shall we say in English, in Bantu and in Afrikaans?); at the kind of place where cynics talk smut, and thieves curse, and soldiers gamble. Because that is where churchmen should be and what churchmanship should be about.

Ron Ferguson

Lord Jesus, it's good to know

Lord Jesus, it's good to know
that you lived in the flesh
walked where we walk, felt what we feel,
got tired, had sore and dirty feet,
needed to eat, and think about
where the next meal was coming from.

But it's even better to know
that you enjoyed your food
the feel of perfume on your skin
the wind on your face, a child in your arms
and the good wine at the wedding.

You didn't mind when people touched you,
even those who were thought of as unclean.
You kissed people with diseases
and laid your head on your friend's shoulder.
Thank you for understanding our bodily pains and pleasures
and for valuing them.

Kathy Galloway

Month 3 Day 30

THE THIRTY-FIRST DAY

'In the midst of death there is life'
(Revelation 21:1–4)

It is hard to imagine that there is anything much worse in our experience today than to endure the agony and the impotence of watching someone we love withering away, devoured before our very eyes by a cancer we are powerless to combat.

Recently I was called to conduct the funeral of a man of 65 years of age, Harry by name, the last two years of whose life had been spent in the increasingly unequal struggle against cancer, and who had for most of these two years been nursed at home gently and devoutly by his wife, Jean.

In preparation for the funeral I had spent an evening sitting chatting to the new widow, getting from her a flavour of the 47 years of married life they had shared. She told me the story of their teenage romance; how, when they were married, he was only 19, an apprentice in the Yards; she, just a messenger girl. How married life had begun in a room in her in-laws home; how they lost a son as a little child; how their other son had thrived, and grown and prospered and had given her and her husband the joy of being grandparents. How her husband had loved his work (he worked in the shipyards all his days), how he had been 'a good Union man'; how he had enjoyed the simple pleasures of a pint and a wee flutter on a Saturday; how he liked to watch the Rangers, and in his later years watch the snooker on TV. He was also a Mason and in the Orange Lodge, but a quiet, decent man who held no truck with the more aggressive expressions of some of his brothers.

Most of all she said, 'Though he was no saint, none of us are, he was a good man and a good father. They told me I was daft getting married at 17, but they were wrong. I'd do it all over again if I got the chance.'

Harry's funeral took place on a Saturday morning and was one of those 'good' funerals where thanksgiving is genuine, where the dignity and the worth of the deceased was evident to all; where mourning, though real, was quietly cushioned by the hope of the Resurrection.

After the funeral service Jean asked me if I was taking my boy to see the Thistle that afternoon. I told her no I wasn't, for I had a wedding to do at three o'clock.

'A wedding,' she said with a sigh. 'Aw, that's nice.' Then, after seeming to think about it for a while she said, 'Would you tell the bride I wish her all the best, and tell her if she's half as lucky as me, she'll be all right.'

So, at the wedding service I told the young bride of the old widow and her wishes for her. The bride cried and afterwards said she just couldn't imagine a nicer greeting on her wedding day. Then she asked if I would take her bouquet after the wedding up to the widow. This I was delighted to do.

Then it was Jean's turn to shed a tear of joy. The bride and the widow, joined together in the shared joy of love. Even though they never met, they made each other's day.

Erik Cramb

Month 3 Day 31

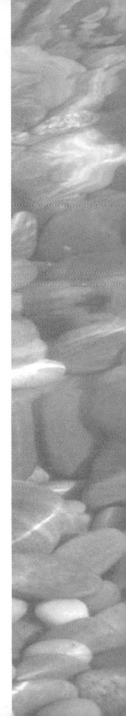

'NEW WAYS TO TOUCH THE HEARTS OF ALL'

And the peacemakers began to dance

Following the landmark ruling on the illegality of Britain's nuclear fleet in the case of the 'Trident Three', many more members took part in the Trident Ploughshares/ Scottish CND Blockade of Faslane Naval Base (February 2001). Community member George Charlton wrote later:

We took the Iona Office, Norman Shanks leading us in the responses. There was something moving and exciting in uttering these words, not on Iona but here at the South Gate of Faslane.

In the prayer for the Iona Community, 'soldiers' of peaceful action and supporters alike prayed for 'courage, faith and cheerfulness' – and for the furthering of the purpose of the Community – 'that hidden things may be revealed to us and new ways found to touch the hearts of all'. So under the darkened skies and the menace of Trident unseen but omnipresent in evil potential we called upon the Master Carpenter to use His practical skills and healing hands so that we who were coming now rough-hewn to this protest against the illegality of Trident in Scottish waters would here be fashioned to a truer beauty of His hand.

And the rain pelted down, and 'the quality of mercy was not strained' as the police cars arrived and the wonderful band of drummers broke into a thunderous drumming of joy and the peace-makers began to dance.

At the North Gate, non-violent resistance was already happening, and we heard the news that the main traffic bringing workers to Faslane Yard had been blocked, so the blockade was holding and the ongoing work of the nuclear weapons system had been disrupted for a little while. The supporters moved to the North Gate soaked but jubilant – and the news was confirmed: ninety had been arrested in resistance to uphold the judgement of Sheriff Margaret Gimblett at Greenock Sheriff Court on 21st October 1999. For we were not breaking the law on 14th February 2001 AD – *we were upholding it*. It was St Valentine's Day and lovers of peace had fastened balloons to the gate and posted the wonderful slogan 'This base is now closed' and 'Trident no more'.

We sang together as people of Civil Resistance: 'No more Trident over me!' Then in defiance of the police who were trying to keep the road free for traffic, young folk began to squat on the wet road, to say *No!* to the government, to the Ministry of Defence, to the market which depends on weapons sales to boost the British economy – *No More Trident!*

George Charlton

Economic Witness

Kingdom values

We know fine well what the Kingdom values are, in broad precept if not in detail, and they're not about narrow religious issues, they're about the basic stuff of human life. They're the stuff of the Sermon on the Mount.

The Kingdom values are about money and possessions and power and sex and violence and security; about war; about how we treat our neighbour; about how we treat our enemy. Fine well we know God's will and we cannot hide behind ignorance.

We know God's will about flowers blooming in wilderness places, about the blind being able to see, the deaf hearing, the lame leaping and dancing and the dumb shouting aloud. It's about drug addicts and AIDS sufferers and the homeless young in 'cardboard cities' being valued and brought in from the cold.

God's will is about those who are 'rubbished' and dismissed being treasured; it's about the powerful being brought to heel; about the first being last and the last first.

It's good news to the poor; about feeding the hungry and clothing the naked; about liberty to the captives and setting free the oppressed; about the time having come when the Lord will save his people.

These are the Kingdom values; that is the Kingdom agenda and we know it well. We cannot hide behind ignorance. We cannot say we do not know … we know, fine well!

Erik Cramb

YOUTH CONCERN

Heavenly bodies

Some friends I was sharing a flat with were joking about what our bodies would be like in heaven – if we were to have 'heavenly bodies':

> I'd be thin, I'd be fit.
> I'd have legs that were self-shaving.
> I'd have self-washing, self-drying,
> self-styling hair. I'd have a smaller nose.
> I'd have bigger eyes and less pointy ears.
> I'd have beautiful skin and no spots.
> I'd have a smaller bum, bigger chest and curly hair.
> No, straight hair. Blonde … no, red.

I laughed and wondered – what if God could hear us now? After God's gone to all that effort to perfect us just exactly the way we were supposed to be … even going to all the effort of counting every hair on our heads … and we come along and decide it's the wrong style, or the wrong colour, or too straight, or too curly. Never satisfied, we want to change everything. God forgive us.

Iona Millar (Youth Associate)

Just a thought

I've spent quite a bit of time in a special care baby unit recently and it's been an amazing experience – one I'll never forget. It really sunk in just how vulnerable the babies are when one of the doctors pointed out that they are so premature that if they get cold they can't even shiver for themselves. When I stopped to think about how much of a struggle every second is for babies, it reminded me just what a miracle birth is and how amazing it is that we're all here today able to do things so much more complex than shivering.

Katie Hacking (Youth Associate)

Month 4 Day 3

THE WORD

Brainstorming the Bible

In the course of this reflecting on the Word of the Lord, members of the (urban theology) group found themselves amazed. In a way they were 'brainstorming the Bible'. They discovered that Paul had written a lot about religious bigotry. In the creation story, they found a story of God at work – and then resting, pleased with the work. So to deny someone the right to work was a denial of part of the image of God in them. In the story of the workers hired in the marketplace to work in the vineyard, they saw the job centre of the first century. These workers, like twentieth-century workers, needed a job because they needed the money – and their needs were the same, whether they had a job or not, whether they were new on the job or not!

But they found that the Bible didn't only speak to and of their own history and context. It didn't only speak to and of their own suffering and hope and vision. It also spoke to and of their ongoing struggles. George MacLeod, the Founder of the Iona Community – itself born out of the struggles of the Depression in Glasgow – wrote, 'Prayer refreshes on the knife-edge.' The urban theology group was being driven back again and again to the Bible, and to prayer, because they were on the knife-edge.

Kathy Galloway

Hospitality and Welcome

Serving in the shop (Isle of Iona)

I met a man from Montana who came into the shop
– wearing silver chains and bracelets,
fat buckles and leather.

He did his shopping over days
and we got to know one another
in transactions and exchanges.

We spoke about the heavy, wet weather.

About Celtic saints and American cowboys.

About alcohol and brokenness,
as he thoughtfully chose gifts,
which I took and carefully
wrapped up in tissue paper
for his family back home.

About the challenge of living
one day at a time
and the comfort and strength
of God's love through prayer.

We blessed one another on his last day of purchases and
there was something light and beautiful
in the jangling way he left walking:
how he came here like a slave and
sailed off like a song.

George MacLeod spoke of *God's great unconditional welcome*. Brother Roger of the Taizé Community writes: 'To be listened to is the beginning of the healing of the soul.'

People came to the Community's shop to spend money of course, to buy books and souvenirs. Customers also came in with a need to share their stories, and something of what they had discovered on Iona; to give thanks to God for time and space to be, and for what they would be taking home with them. There was sometimes a rich exchange.

With so many people coming to Iona, in the summer especially, it could sometimes be a real challenge for staff to stay open. Community life was crowded and busy – life in all its fullness.

After a full day of work and worship, I went home to Cul Dunsmeorach and wrote the following prayer.

Prayer

All-embracing, all-loving God,
help me to remain open to the demands
of welcome.

All-accepting, all-seeing Christ,
help me to recognise you in
each tourist and pilgrim.

Holy spirit
present everywhere always,
enter into me

Help me serve
with cheerfulness
humility
gentleness
patience.

Neil Paynter

THIS IS THE DAY

The kingdom is near

Here,
among the pots and pans,
Now,
kneaded and rolled into apple pie
fragrant and warm and spicy.
Here,
around the kitchen table,
Now,
present to all the hurts and injustices.
Here,
in the dance,
weaving patterns of conviviality and resistance.
Now, open house, open hearts.
Here,
listening, respect, encouragement,
Now,
right relationship is not postponed.
Here and now.
Only this.
It is enough.

Kathy Galloway

THE IONA EXPERIENCE

A place of hope

'A place of hope,'
they say:
and in their thousands
they journey, year by year,
to this tiny island
on the margins of Europe.
Sunswept and windswept,
yet always deeply
a place of transformation.
A sacred spot on earth:
a pilgrim's place
of light and shadow
energy and challenge.

We need you, Iona,
with your alternative vision,
with your ever-present questions
your often uncomfortable silence.

For you are a place of prayer,
of Christ's abiding:

weaving a rainbow of meaning
through the endless busyness of our days,
holding together the frayed threads
of our fleeting devotion,
opening a path for healing
and for peace.
Not momentary healing
nor easy faith,
but struggle, commitment,
and an ongoing conversion
are your gifts for
our broken yet beautiful lives.

Peter Millar

LIFE IN COMMUNITY

Reflection from Iona

Well, here we are, getting ready to start another season. And I find myself thinking about all the amazing, wonderful new people I'm about to have the privilege of welcoming and getting to know, and sharing life in community with – new volunteers, residents, Abbey and MacLeod Centre guests. I think of the arrival of all these wonderful new people with real anticipation and excitement, but also with a feeling of dread. Dread of all the sheer physical stamina and emotional energy it will take to welcome so many different people and, most of all, dread of another season full of goodbyes – dread of opening up and exposing myself to grief and loss. It's what people who come to live and work here have one of the greatest difficulties with. The so many goodbyes. Over and over, again and again.

One hundred and fifteen volunteers passed through Iona last year. One hundred and fifteen volunteers, twenty-four residents, five thousand guests, one hundred and fifty thousand pilgrims and seekers, tourists and day trippers. It's the nature of this place, the comings and goings, the ferrying over and away.

I find myself dwelling mainly on the pain of saying goodbye to the volunteers. Volunteers come to Iona from all over the world, and live and work at the island centres for from six to twelve weeks.

Six to twelve weeks is just enough time to get to know somebody here. Just enough time to make a friend. It doesn't take long. Iona is 'a thin place' as George MacLeod said, and just as the barrier between the spiritual and the material is like tissue paper in places, emotional and social barriers between people can thin and dissolve and tear away. There's an intensity to living, working and worshipping together that can quickly open people up, and sometimes make them feel vulnerable. There's an intimacy to living on an island. An unbelievable amazing feeling of talking to people who care about the same things as you do; exciting exchange of ideas and experiences. There's the magic and wonder and beauty of nature all around which can suddenly open people's eyes to the sacred beauty and uniqueness of others around them – emotion of the sea, churning, swelling, flowing; sun glowing warmly on the red rocks of Mull; tangled seaweed tossed up; freedom to be of the wind dancing. There's an overwhelming feeling of connectedness that can make you want to run up and embrace others as brother and sister. Overwhelming feeling of your insignificance. Aloneness – against the great crashing sea, billion-starred sky – that fills you with the need, and the courage, to reach out.

I find myself thinking of volunteers I've got to know in my time here. And their faces and spirits flash, and the brilliant times we shared: midnight conversations about life and God and love and dreams; climbing Dun I to watch the sunrise of our hearts; working together and building support; arguments and reconciliations and forgiveness and growth; walking to the north end to touch the sea and say prayers to the stars; laughing together at the disco; crying together at healing services.

I think of all we shared and how difficult it has been to let those people and special times go. And about going through it all again: another joyful dance and storm-tossed trudge of another season on Iona. Another one hundred and fifteen hellos and goodbyes. The sick feeling every Wednesday morning when we straggle down to the jetty, hung over from emotion and goodbye drinks and the disco-till-you-drop. Wrench of last hugs as the ferry slowly opens up its stupid metal mouth and swallows up cars, bicycles, friends. Doing 'the Mexican wave' as the ferry ploughs and punches away out into the sound. And grows ever smaller. Standing there in the tug of wind, holding flimsy addresses and the tight feeling of absence tucked in the pit of your stomach. Then, turning around and heading back to work; later that same day, welcoming a clutch of new volunteers, who arrive off the ferry to fill the gaps and holes.

The experience certainly keeps you re-learning the lesson of change and impermanence. But to live it is hard. You start not wanting to get too close to people because they're just going to leave you. You protect yourself. Dive into your work, dive into your room nights, dive into your cell of self. And for me it's all too symbolic of the greater comings and goings in life. With some volunteers who leave it's like: there goes my grandmother whom I watched die in a hospital bed two springtimes ago. Leaving me again. Sailing off. There's my lover whom I spent ten years with. Waving. Then standing with her back turned – like a blank wall. Like a closed door. (My ex-partner actually came to visit me here last year, and left in a sea of faces one Wednesday. And so now every Wednesday I recall that day.) You're reminded again and again, here, how nothing is permanent and all is flowing change.

And so I walk alone to work down past the sea and think how terrifying and freeing that thought is. Go into the Abbey to pray, thinking how nothing is permanent except maybe my relationship with God. And so I tuck up in that warm, loving, secure feeling a moment. *Do not be afraid* – but feel afraid. Lose it, try to find it again. But God doesn't live in an abbey anyway. God lives in the world, in people – in their smiles, and laughter, and tears, and holy spirits. And I think how maybe the best way to say goodbye is not goodbye but *Bless you. You are not mine, I am not yours. Let us embrace but not cling. Let us let go and go on, on our separate journeys. Feel the grief and joy and adventure of living. Live life with a fullness, welcoming newness, the arrival of each moment.*

Well, here I am, ready to start a new season. And I find myself thinking about all the gifted moments I've shared here, and how it's all worth it. I think of all the amazing, wonderful new people I'm soon to have the privilege of meeting, and I feel a real buzz of anticipation and excitement. Openness dawning over the dread. I wonder who I'll meet here at the crossroads this time; sit down and listen to; break bread with.

> May God's goodness be yours,
> And well, and seven times well, may you spend your lives:
> May you be an isle in the sea,
> May you be a hill on the shore,
> May you be a star in the darkness,
> May you be a staff to the weak;
> May the love Christ Jesus gave fill every heart for you;
> May the love Christ Jesus gave fill you for every one.

Neil Paynter, a former member of the Resident Group on Iona

WOMEN

If Christ cannot be seen in women

I began my journey of knowing God in the feminine through the Holy Spirit as the Lady, and this seemed to be at Her invitation and in response to my need. But I found this not enough. I wanted to know God as both feminine and masculine, in every person of the Trinity. The use of the word 'Goddess' is dualistic, revealing God as male. 'God/dess' is only a written expression of the Divine. For me we would be post-patriarchy when we teach, preach and pray moving between masculine and feminine pronouns and images – without comment, without people saying, 'I can see you need it,' or 'I think of God as love,' who then see no inconsistency in saying 'Lord', 'he', etc. To my surprise, as I thought about it, I found that within what I knew of the Lady there was a Christian Trinity: Mother; Christa; Lady Wisdom, not just the Holy Spirit.

I knew God as Mother, one who made me, and this has made knowing God as Father much richer. There will always be times in the life of faith when we need to turn as a child to a parent of whatever gender, but it has been challenging to know of God as birthing, pushing, with perfect timing, as well as the more familiar nurturer.

I am glad to know Jesus as saviour and friend, to know Him as the Christ, but I need my sister Christ also. Her breast-feeding of me at a difficult time physically and spiritually has been formative. Women Christians were crucified and thrown to the lions as well as men. Christ was in them all, and *if Christ cannot be seen in women, then women cannot be Christian.*

Chris Polhill

Wholly God

If God were a woman
I would be much braver
when it comes
to the heart of the matter;
or rather, when it comes
to matters of the heart.

If God were a woman
I would throw my inhibitions
to the wind.
I would sparkle
and toss and bounce
with laughter and the guts of love
as the sole means of
communication.

If God were a woman
life would be
as light as the top soil,
as free as the froth, or the frost,
which come and go with the seasons
and the tides and
make a slave of
no one.

If God were a woman
life would be round and full
and tears would conquer fear
which would tremble,
then disappear
in the presence of
such splendid
wholeness.

If God were a woman
life would be complete.
Nothing more. No show.
No great crusade. No mission.
For God would be complete
in you, in me, that's all.

Ruth Harvey

PRAYER

Everyone can pray

So many people think that it is only holy and pious sorts of folk that pray, and that it is unnatural. But that is just nonsense. If you believe in God, it is most unnatural *not* to pray.

But what is even more important to remember is that we have to act as well as pray, if our prayers are going to be answered as God wants them to be answered. For instance, King Hezekiah prayed that Jerusalem should have a better water supply, but it did not come by magic. Hezekiah had, as we say, to take his jacket off, roll up his sleeves, and dig the tunnel.

I am going to mention one more kind of prayer, and I often think that this is the most important of all, and that is the prayer of thanks. There is simply no limit to the things we have to say thank you for. There is the sun and moon, the sunshine and rain, the sea and rivers, the birds and animals, in fact the whole of nature. Then there are our parents, our friends, our health and strength.

One of the things I am always thanking God for is that I am alive at this time of history. I think this is a marvellous age and I am grateful just to be alive and able to help in the tremendous jobs that need to be done.

Roger Gray

Think of the Maker

Leader: In the beginning, God made the world.
Let us give thanks for all that God has made.

Think of a time when you saw that the world is beautiful …
Think of a sunset over the hills,
    or sunrise over a sleeping city.
Think of a running river,
    or stars shining on a dark sea.
Think of light flashing on a puddle,
    or of geraniums growing in a window-box.
Think of a time when you saw that the world is beautiful
        – and give thanks.

Think of a time when you found pleasure in your body …
Think of walking in the wind, or digging a garden.
Think of dancing till dawn, or climbing a mountain.
Think of giving birth to a child,
    or of holding someone you love.
Think of a time when you found pleasure in your body
        – and give thanks.

Think of a time when you learned something new about life …
Think of understanding something that has always been a mystery
    or of seeing someone else in a different light.
Think of discovering a talent you never knew you had,
    or of listening to a good idea.
Think of knowing what is important to you,
    or of believing that some things matter more than others.
Think of a time when you learned something new about life
        – and give thanks.

Think of a time when your spirit was refreshed …
Think of a song that moved you to tears,
    or of a prayer that inspired you to act.
Think of laughter shared with friends,
    or care of your family.
Think of a stranger who made you feel welcome,
    or of someone who said, 'I love you.'
Think of a time when your spirit was refreshed
        – and give thanks.

Think of a time when you were in despair …
Think of feeling alone in a roomful of people
    or of being unwanted by even one person.
Think of being ashamed because you've hurt someone,
    or of being awkward because you misjudged a situation.
Think of being worn with worry or anxiety,
    or of knowing that your life is a sorry, disgusting mess.
Think of a time when you were in despair
    – then think of the suffering, forgiving,
        changing love of Jesus
            – and give thanks.

The world belongs to the Lord,
    Think of the Maker – and give thanks.

Kathy Galloway

Month 4 Day 10

JUSTICE AND PEACE

Hand in hand

Surely salvation is at hand.
Steadfast love and faithfulness will meet,
righteousness and peace will kiss each other.
Psalm 85:8–13

Each morning in worship we imagine justice and peace joining hands. It is a powerful possibility. If that happened, after centuries of war and injustice, how would the world be changed? It is a memorable image, like the marathon runners who chose to cross the finishing line together, hand in hand. In the Revised English Bible justice and peace embrace. In the Revised Standard Version (and the AV) they kiss. We shouldn't lose sight of the passion – and the passionate yearning.

> God our Saviour,
> walk toward us on a path of peace:
> encourage us, in our loneliness and yearning,
> take us in your arms and lift us up,
> enable us to receive your goodness and grace,
> to perceive your glory already around us,
> here and now, and to believe
> that justice and peace
> can indeed go hand in hand.
> Amen

Jan Sutch Pickard

THE INTEGRITY OF CREATION

Oh the life of the world

Oh the life of the world is a joy and a treasure,
unfolding in beauty the green-growing tree,
the changing of seasons in mountain and valley
the stars and the bright restless sea.

Oh the life of the world is a fountain of goodness
overflowing in labour and passion and pain,
in the sound of the city and the silence of wisdom,
in the birth of a child once again.

Oh the life of the world is the source of our healing.
It rises in laughter and wells up in song;
it springs from the care of the poor and the broken
and refreshes where justice is strong.

So give thanks for the life and give love to the Maker
and rejoice in the gift of the bright risen Son.
And walk in the peace and the power of the Spirit
till the days of our living are done.

Kathy Galloway

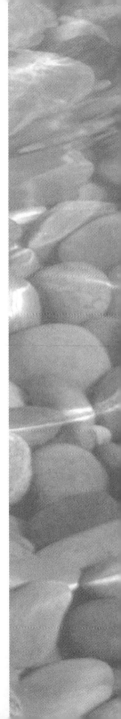

COLUMBAN CHRISTIANITY & THE CELTIC TRADITION

In the footsteps of Columba today

There is so much to treasure in the heritage of Columba and the Celtic Christian tradition. The scholars may debate the details, but the main thrusts and themes are beyond dispute. What was distinctive was not only Columba's holiness … there was also a wholeness, a roundness and a rootedness about his faith. Columba's life was grounded in the conviction that God's loving purpose encompasses and permeates the whole of life, is relevant to every human need and situation: and that is why the Gospel is literally 'good news'. God is to be discovered, experienced, encountered not only in contemplative tranquillity, not only in remote, beautiful Hebridean islands; but also thoroughly down-to-earth, in the hurly-burly of life, in corporate worship, in the ebb and flow of relationships, in grappling with the struggles, tensions and issues of the day. Contrary to what is often perceived and purveyed as 'Celtic spirituality', often self-indulgent, essentially individualistic, the true Columban tradition is about engagement and not escape. It holds spiritual and social concerns inextricably together. It is indeed a rich legacy, a formidable challenge for those who seek to walk in the footsteps of Columba today.

Norman Shanks

Blessing

May God be a bright flame before you,
be a guiding star above you,
be a smooth path below you,
be a kindly shepherd behind you,
today, tomorrow and for ever.
Amen.

St Columba

RACISM

Dropping the adjectives

You call us
bogus asylum-seekers,
fraudulent claimants
promiscuous homosexuals
pretend families
rebellious youth
manipulative children
strident women.

How about
dropping the adjectives?
Then we would be
asylum-seekers,
claimants,
homosexuals,
families,
youth,
children,
women.

Better still,
let's change them.

We could be called
desperate asylum-seekers,
genuine claimants
happy homosexuals
real families
challenging youth
hurting children
assertive women

after all, one word's as good as another …

Isn't it?

Alix Brown

COMMUNITY

Communities of hope are always breaking open

Genuine intimacy is a precious and gracious gift. It is rare enough in our depersonalised society for us not to take it for granted. And yet, though it is a gift of community, it is not to be equated with community. Intimacy is formed in a 'gestalt', a context with defined boundaries, within which it is safe to be vulnerable, open, and let the masks slip. The intimacy which Jesus enjoyed with his disciples was a natural part of close relations with a group of people over a period of time.

The disciples loved their intimacy with Jesus. They wanted to hold on to it. They grieved for its loss after his death. But they did not understand what he had shown them at their last meal together. Intimacy is always exclusive. The boundaries that make it possible, that include us in, always keep others out. This is a perennial problem in churches. We live in a continual tension between those who are on the inside and those who are on the outside, not just of the church itself, but of the various smaller groupings that co-exist within the church.

And sometimes we confuse intimacy with being a community of hope. We cannot deny the need and the giftedness of intimacy. It is part of being human. It affirms us, values us. And yet the calling of communities of hope is to accept that affirmation and value – that gift – and take it out into the world. Not to think that we can do without boundaries, but to be ready to break open our common life and share it. It is a constant forming and reforming, and we often experience it as a kind of death. But it is death that brings new life, it is bread broken to be shared. Communities of hope are always breaking open.

Kathy Galloway

PILGRIMAGE

Pilgrims or planners

We are either 'pilgrims' or 'planners'. 'Planners' spend their time trying to match up and fit into their lifestyle goals and priorities set by others, and measure the value of their social achievements in terms of material success. 'Pilgrims' on the other hand cope with the unpredictability of life, accept human vulnerability and see life's ups and downs in terms of opportunities for human growth.

Norman Shanks

To finish

Pilgrim God,
our shoes are filled with stones,
our feet are blistered and bleeding,
our faces are stained with tears.

As we stumble and fall
may we know your presence
in the bleeding and in the tears
and in the healing and the laughter
of our pilgrimage.

Kate McIlhagga

SEXUALITY

Christ from a different starting point

What if we were to read Christ from a different starting point? If we believe that Jesus reveals God to us, and God in relation to humankind, then what I see is not a petulant, prohibitive God, but a divine permissiveness which desires nothing more than our wellbeing, whose pleasure it is to give us the kingdom (or perhaps even the Garden). In this reading, there is an invitation to right relationship, to something fuller, freer and more satisfying than we have previously known.

One of the losses of our present guardedness is that the nature and extent of relationships can very easily become terribly reduced, leaving us too often with only the sexual relationship, the nuclear family and the single person bearing the weight of all our human needs and desires – and all of these cracking under that burden. This is an emotionally emaciated condition.

For Jesus, there was no such thing as a single person. There was only the community, and those who, for some reason, had been excluded or isolated from the community – foreigners, outcasts of every kind, destitute and homeless people, those in mental distress, 'harlots'. These he brought back into relationship with the community, in a series of exchanges which transformed people's consciousness about themselves, about others and about God. Exclusion against one's will was wrong relationship for Jesus.

Though these exchanges were different, some joyful, some sorrowful, all of them seem to me to share certain characteristics. Firstly, every one of them is marked by a generosity of heart and spirit, by going beyond where legality requires them to go. Secondly, they are spontaneous, they leap out in a self-forgetful way, whether in gladness or compassion or care. Thirdly, that spontaneity is drawn out by some deep respect for, or delight in, the otherness of the other, in who they are. Fourthly, the exchange is one of freedom – there is no coercion in the response, whether through fear or law or the desire for approval. And, finally, something changes for the better because of the exchange. All – whether giver or receiver – gain. And the integration of the excluded one into an extended and wider community, back into relationship, is the context of the exchange. The exchange is redemptive. For Jesus, part of the consequence of love, of the outrageous and subversive transformation of relationship, was indeed suffering. It may be a consequence for us. That is no reason to idealise and idolise suffering. Why would we desire anyone to suffer for us? To love us – that's a different thing.

The community that Jesus created was one of free and autonomous co-equals: 'not servants but friends' (*John 15:15*). In our autonomous and mobile society of individuals, in which traditional communities based on geography, work, class or religion are increasingly breaking down, perhaps attention to the structures, values and practices that affirm and rebuild inclusive, just and compas-sionate communities would bring us into a more diverse experience of relation-ship and a more natural context for relaxing and taking a few risks. Perhaps we need to discover new ways of being *human* together in order to find new ways of being men and women, or women and women, or men and men together. Perhaps there is a reweaving needed of the web of life that itself supports us through the times we betray and hurt one another, as we inevitably do.

Our deepest hungers – for acceptance, for affirmation of our lovability and our value regardless of achievement – may find nourishment in one lifelong part-ner. They may find nourishment in a community of relationships. They may find nourishment in celibacy, or even in great solitude, in commitment to justice-making or in creative work. People are different, and should be allowed to remain so. And yet there is that in us which remains unfilled and unfulfilled, even in the best relationship or the happiest family. Religious people have described this as the yearning for God, others as the longing for connection with all that is, with the ground of our being. Perhaps it is the desire for our truest and deepest selves, the self which wants to be whole, to come home, the self to which we are over and over again unfaithful.

Kathy Galloway

HEALING

Renaming others

One of my obsessions in life is persuading people that they can sing. One in four adults believe they can't sing, simply because at a vulnerable time in their lives someone – a parent, friend or teacher – told them they couldn't. And they live under the shadow of that pronouncement. They sometimes even give themselves a title – the groaner, the crow, the drone.

I don't believe that God would ask us to sing him a new song unless he knew it was possible. So I try to persuade people to forget what was said to them in the past, and believe that they have the voice of an apprentice angel.

I was teaching a course one weekend in Edinburgh. To this came some people from one of the most deprived public housing areas in Europe. Among them was a woman called Rose who challenged my assumption that everyone can sing because she had a voice like a corncrake in the off-season.

However, I persevered. We sang a whole lot of different kinds of music that weekend, including chants from the Russian Orthodox Church. Nothing would have even vaguely corresponded to Rose's usual musical tastes, which were firmly Country and Western.

I was astounded to get a phone call from her two weeks later, asking if I would come on a Friday evening to the church where she worshipped in order to help a group of marginalised people to pray. I arrived in this most desperate of areas and was taken into a room full of people whose faces and demeanour told a thousand stories. Several were recovering alcoholics; some were recently out of prison; some were parents whose children had been removed from them by courts.

I was reeling internally, wondering how on earth to begin, when Rose said: 'There'll be no difficulty with the singing. I told them two weeks ago that I was an apprentice angel and that if I could sing, so could they. We can all do the *Kyrie Eleison*.'

So, in that direst of neighbourhoods, and in the dingiest of church halls, we lit a candle and dimmed the room lights, and I invited people as they wished to speak to Jesus about what was on their hearts as if he were sitting next to them. And after each prayer, after each deep heart-wrung and heart-rending prayer, this fragile company of nothings and nobodies sang a Russian Orthodox *Kyrie*, 'Lord Have Mercy', with abject devotion, thanks to a wee woman with a voice like a corncrake who believed she was an apprentice angel.

I don't imagine that this side of time I will ever again be privileged to share in prayer which was as close to heaven, and to join in singing which had the integrity of an angelic choir.

You see this woman … she is a daughter of Abraham.

You see this man … he is a son of Abraham.

You see yourselves … you are children of the living God.

That is your name.

That is your identity.

Live up to it.

John L. Bell

Month 4 Day 18

SOCIAL ACTION

'All good things in the world come from fools with faith'

One of my favourite old Hollywood films, often shown on television around Christmas, is a James Stewart black-and-white classic, *Mr Smith Goes to Washington*. It is a kind of fairy-tale about a decent man in small-town America, who in the pursuit of honesty and public concern is precipitated into politics and ends up in Washington, on the threshold of the White House. One memorable line of dialogue has stuck in my mind: 'All good things in the world come from fools with faith.' The distinguished anthropologist Margaret Mead put the same thought in a slightly different way that challenges us to commitment, and also reassures us in our continuing quest for social and political change: 'Never doubt that a small group of thoughtful citizens can change the world. Indeed it is the only thing that ever has.'

Norman Shanks

CHURCH RENEWAL

My vision of church

Over the last two years a group of five of us have been meeting once a month, to eat together, to study the Bible and to pray. We choose themes for study that reflect our concerns and interests. Our prayers come out of these discussions and are made in the form of silence, songs, painting together, lighting candles. In the sharing of our concerns we listen hard to one another.

Over the years together we have developed a degree of trust and honesty which enhances this sharing. My vision of church is that groups of people can meet with joy and anticipation, share their concerns honestly with each other, share food, and offer these concerns, hopes and fears in the presence of each other to God. My vision of ministry is that we in the churches will recognise those who have the gift of enabling this process to happen and will encourage small, seemingly insignificant 'gatherings' like this to grow.

My vision of church is that individuals can be freed to spend time alone with God and not feel they have to verify that freedom on a Sunday morning. My vision of ministry is that a climate of self-expression will be enabled to grow within the context of a rooted, communal ministry.

My vision of church is that we will recognise Christ in the most unlikely places and there be able to say, 'Ah, church!' My vision of ministry is that it will be a vehicle through which the Bible and other wise texts can come alive, drawing on the insights and experience of those with little or no formal training who never-theless walk in Christ's path.

Ruth Harvey

What gives me hope

I'm still not sure whether the traditional church can have any relevance for me in the future. Is it right to struggle on, trying to work for change in the local parishes, which is, after all, where the people are – or is that a waste of valuable energy when there are so many important things to do in the world? Would it be better for the traditional structures to collapse so that new forms of Christian community can emerge? Would opting out of the structures mean that we leave them to the traditionalists or the growing numbers of conservative evangelicals in the churches who seem afraid to ask the questions and cling to the traditional because it appears to offer security? These are a few of the questions. What gives me hope is that I know I am not the only one asking them.

Lynda Wright

Prayer

O Christ, you are within each of us.
It is not just the interior of these walls;
it is our own inner being you have renewed.
We are your temple not made with hands.
We are your body.
If every wall should crumble, and every church decay,
we are your habitation.
Nearer are you than breathing, closer than hands and feet.
Ours are the eyes with which you, in the mystery,
look out with compassion on the world.
Yet we bless you for this place,
for your directing of us, your redeeming of us,
and your indwelling.
Take us outside, O Christ, outside holiness,
out to where soldiers curse and nations clash
at the crossroads of the world.
So shall this building continue to be justified.
We ask it for your own name's sake.
Amen

George MacLeod

WORSHIP

The religious moment flowers from the practical

Our engagement is constantly driving us into prayer. As George MacLeod, the founder of the Community, wrote: 'There are evenings when our prayer life is refreshing: but, analysed, they turn out to be the times when the pressures have been so weighty that you have simply had to go with them to God. But this is precisely the recovery of the knife-edge. The religious moment flowers from the practical.' Nowhere is this more true than on the knife-edge of political and social engagement.

Many of the most significant acts of worship for members of the Community on the mainland have not been in churches. They have been outdoors, on demonstrations and marches and picket-lines, outside military bases and the Ministry of Defence, in city squares and at embassies. Equally important, though perhaps less dramatically, they have been in homes and community centres, in schools and factories and hospitals, all the places where people struggle on a knife-edge and we among them. At the very least, we can take our bodies, and our prayers, and say with them, 'I beg to differ'; we can witness to our conviction that 'it is better to light a candle than to curse the darkness'.

Kathy Galloway

An Adomnán liturgy of celebration

To mark 'Carnival' at Faslane (Trident nuclear missile submarine base)
13 May 2000

St Adomnán of Iona is best known as the biographer of St Columba. However, in his own time he was recognised as the author of the Cain Adomnán, or 'Law of the Innocents'. Known as 'the first law in heaven and earth for the protection of women', Adomnán's Law extended to children and clergy, and is an early attempt to protect con-combatants. It is a precursor of the Geneva Conventions and the United Nations' Declaration of Human Rights. It was said that instead of carrying a sword into battle, Adomnán carried a bell, 'the bell of Adomnán's anger', which he rang out against injustice and the tyrants of his day.[1]

Part one: A time for diagnosis

Leader 1:   Now is the time to live, to come to the Creator, to sing and dance to the Lord who frees us from fear, to help create a better world with the Spirit of Love. *(Bell rings once)*

(Short silence)

Leader 1:   Let us invite the whole world to join us in praise.
All: The time has come. *(Bell)*

Leader 2:   Let us acknowledge our failures to live as God's children.
All: The time has come. *(Bell)*

Leader 3:   For our willingness to use Trident, we seek God's pardon.
All: The time has come. *(Bell)*

Leader 4:   For our failure to amend our lives and share with others the fruits of creation, we ask God's pardon.
All: The time has come. *(Bell)*

| Leader 1: | For our reluctance as a society to acknowledge our sickness and accept healing, we ask God's pardon. |
| All: | The time has come. *(Bell)* |

(Short silence)

| Leader 2: | Many times we have come to this place and seen the horror it inflicts on our land. We know what worse horrors it could inflict on other people's lands, on our God-given planet, should the weaponry deployed here ever be used. We have often used both Scripture and Adomnán's Law to remind those who work here of their responsibility, and ours, to both God and humanity. Today we come to remind ourselves, as well as those who work here, of our responsibility to heal the sickness of our society, to heal this place and restore Faslane Bay again to a health spa, a place of celebration. We hear again Ezekiel, but listen to the message of responsibility to celebrate life. |

| Reader: | *(Reading from the Prophet Ezekiel, Chapter 37:1–14)* |

(Short silence)

Part two: A time for healing

Leader 2:	We seek to heal this place of Death
All:	Deep peace to you *(Bell)*
Leader 3:	We seek to heal all those who work here from the sickness of fear
All:	Deep peace to you *(Bell)*
Leader 4:	We seek to heal the world's hunger by redistributing resources
All:	Deep peace to you *(Bell)*
Leader 1:	We seek to heal the environment of all that harms life
All:	Deep peace to you *(Bell)*

Month 4 Day 21

| Leader 2: | We seek to heal and make whole all who would hold life truly a gift from God |
| All: | Deep peace to you   *(Bell)* |

(Short silence)

| Leader 3: | We have often rung the Bell of Adomnán in this place as a symbolic reminder of that law honoured by our Celtic ancestors and by those who walked in the traditions of Iona. That Bell often was known as a sign of condemnation of those who failed to keep the law. It is also the case, however, that in Celtic tradition, bells, and particularly Adomnán's Bell, were often used as a sign of healing. We invite you now to ring your own small bells, as Adomnán's heirs, as a symbol of your will to bring healing on this place and on all who are present today. |

(Time for lots of bells to be rung)

Part three: A time for celebration

Leader 4:	Most religious traditions stress the importance of sharing. Many also see the deep value of sharing a meal. In the simple act of partaking of the same gifts of the earth, people are bound together in a common act of humanity, a sacred trust. As we come to this place, we are witnesses to the imbalance of our sharing of the earth's resources. In the tradition of the Christian community of Columba and Adomnán, we hear again of a great symbolic act of sharing.
Reader:	*(Reading from Gospel of Mark 6:30–44)*
Leader 1:	We may not be able to feed five thousand here today. But we invite you to share symbolically in what we have. These gifts are already an act of trust, an act of sharing. Since Trident Ploughshares 2000

got under way, some of the Adomnán of Iona Affinity Group have been visited regularly by the Lothian and Borders CID (Criminal Investigation Department). On each occasion we have shared hospitality with them. On the last two visits, they kindly brought provisions for our 'working afternoon tea'. We could not consume all the fragments of the last session, and, as they themselves said, 'There is enough to share with your friends.' We now invite you to share in their gift to us all. A gift of friendship. A gift of mutual trust and respect. A gift of a pledge of a fully healed future.

(We share biscuits and juice with, firstly, any police, then each other and any of the folk who are around us.)

Conclusion: Litany of celebration
(with acknowledgement to Norman C. Habel[2])

Leader 1: Today the Lord steps into the air once more, to taste its colour and feel its songs. He inhales the thoughts of children, the hopes of yesterday, the fantasies of tomorrow, and he wonders whether his children are too old to celebrate their dreams.

All: Let us spin him our dreams.

Leader 2: Someday soon people here will celebrate life every day.

All: We would do it now.

Leader 3: Someday soon people will turn this place into a holiday camp.

All: Turn the Ship Lift into a cafeteria.

Leader 4: Someday soon people will glimpse the face of God in each other.

All: Use the eyes of friends in place of mirrors.

Leader 5: Someday soon people will sink their teeth into politics for peace.

All: Share their food with the hungry.

Leader 1: Someday soon people will turn all bombs into beachballs.

All: All Trident missiles into railway trains.

Leader 2: Someday soon people will slow down and wait for God

---

All:	Run and dance through Faslane base with bare feet.
Leader 3:	Someday soon people will laugh in the restored spring grass
All:	Dance in the nuclear-free waves.
Leader 4:	Someday soon people will celebrate Easter every day.
All:	And hang Christmas banners from the moon.
Leader 5:	Someday soon people will live like that.
All:	But we plan to start right now! Amen! Right now!

(We share our balloons with everybody, draw on them etc., but slowly move off to our chosen place to continue the 'party'.)

Notes on the service:

At some point in the Office – we are very flexible – we read or proclaim part of the 'Cain Adomnán' or Adomnán's Law[3], paragraphs 28, 27, 33, 34 and sometimes part of 35. We conclude with section 21 in full. We generally give a short introduction to its date and significance in its own time. We then try to add to that its relevance for us as Iona Community members or 'Heirs of Adomnán'. Depending on which bells we have, they are rung either at this point or during the action itself. For the opening of the campaign back in August 1998, we had large pictures of victims of Hiroshima lined up across the gate. We had been lent the Abbey copy of the Adomnán Bell – a gift of the Corrymeela Community. We managed to create a silence and then stood in front of each portrait and simply rang the bell for each one. It was very moving. Just for the record, after the litany of celebration, the 'party' continued until members of the Adomnán Group and others were arrested.

The Adomnán Affinity Group (Maire-Colette Wilkie)

Month 4 Day 21

WORK

The Gospel and the physical

The Iona Community is concerned with the building of an Abbey. It is also concerned with the impact of the Gospel on other structures than stone – the impact of the Gospel on the international structure, on the industrial and the economic structure. We believe 'the whole creation groaneth, waiting for the revealing of the sons of God'. It is also concerned with the ancient gift to the Church of the power to heal. You say it is concerned with a lot of different things? Precisely, no. All these are one thing – *the impact of the Gospel on the physical.*

Nov. 1939 (Iona Community Archives)

The rebuilding of lives

'We are still, as a community, in the process of rebuilding – in the business of rebuilding, if you like, even though the reconstruction, the restoration, of the Abbey was completed in 1967. We see ourselves as playing a part in the rebuilding of lives – the accompanying of people on their own personal journeys, seeking to contribute to the rebuilding of the Church, and seeking to play a part, too, in the reshaping of wider society through social and political change.

'The Iona Community has always been interested in spiritual matters – in fact, seeing spiritual matters as being not distinct from material or secular matters. 'God permeates everything.' So we promote an integrated approach to spirituality, saying that spirituality is about engagement: about engaging with people, about engaging with the issues of our time and engaging with God.'

Norman Shanks

CALLED TO BE ONE

Think global – act local

Here is a Christmas card which I received on 11 December, 1989 from George MacLeod, the founder of the Iona Community:

> If you wish to go well in January then
> A. Every Sunday morning read St Matthew's Gospel Chapter 5
> B. Every Sunday evening read St Matthew's Gospel Chapter 6
> C. Every month take communion at the nearest celebration of Communion regardless of its denomination. Christ has only one Church and you are a member of its body by reason of your Baptism.
> D. Read now Colossians 3:1–17
> Have a good Xmas,
> George

Colossians 3 paints a global picture of a cosmic Christ in whose world there cannot be Greek or Jew, circumcised and uncircumcised, barbarian, Scythian, slave and free man. It gives the wide ecumenical vision of Christ as all and in all. Matthew 5 and 6, the Sermon on the Mount, applies that vision to particular local situations and circumstances such as going a second mile, loving your enemy and not being anxious about tomorrow.

For George MacLeod, the global had to be rooted in the local and this rooting found its focus in communion at the nearest church. The fullness of the universal Church is manifested in the local eucharistic community.

For George MacLeod the work of the Iona Community was not what happened on Iona, nor what happened in plenary meetings of members, but what was happening in the local areas where community members were living. In other words, there was no point in coming to Iona to make idealistic affirmations about loving God, if you could not love your neighbour back at the ranch.

Murdoch MacKenzie

Hope for the world

Leader: In quietness and darkness,
in peace and confusion,
Jesus Christ wants to make his home
and meet his friends.
He is the light of life:

ALL: HE IS THE HOPE FOR THE WORLD.

Leader: In him there is neither Jew nor Gentile,
neither Roman Catholic nor Protestant,

ALL: ALL ARE ONE IN JESUS CHRIST.

Leader: He is the light of life:

ALL: HE IS THE HOPE FOR THE WORLD.

Month 4 Day 23

Leader: In him there is neither black nor white,
            neither north nor south:
ALL: ALL ARE ONE IN JESUS CHRIST.

Leader: He is the light of life:
ALL: HE IS THE HOPE FOR THE WORLD.

Leader: In him is neither male nor female,
            neither master nor servant:
ALL: ALL ARE ONE IN JESUS CHRIST.

Leader: He is the light of life:
ALL: HE IS THE HOPE FOR THE WORLD.

Leader: In him there is neither rich nor poor,
            neither middle class nor working class:
ALL: ALL ARE ONE IN JESUS CHRIST.

Leader: He is the light of life
ALL: HE IS THE HOPE FOR THE WORLD.

MISSION

An enormous need

'The way the folk in the urban theology group worked became known because it was used by poor communities in Latin America. It gave them a global connection.'

Kathy Galloway

'That way of being the church, or of doing theology, meant that the church changed from being an institution that looked first and foremost after itself, into being something which sought to be a sign of God's Kingdom. I think we're part of a world church – and it's one of the things, in this country, we're beginning to recognise. And that rather than the riches of our tradition and heritage going from here to other parts of the world, there is now an enormous need for the riches of other parts of the world to influence and to shape our understanding of mission and our understanding of Church.'

Martin Johnstone

Sent by the Lord am I

Sent by the Lord am I;
my hands are ready now
to make the earth the place
in which the kingdom comes.
Sent by the Lord am I;
my hands are ready now
to make the earth the place
in which the kingdom comes

The angels cannot change
a world of hurt and pain
into a world of love,
of justice and of peace.
The task is mine to do,
to set it really free.
Oh, help me to obey;
help me to do your will.

Jorge Maldonado

Month 4 Day 24

THE POOR AND DISADVANTAGED

An offence to God

We may learn from the poor, first and foremost, about what it means to be truly human in the world. The broken, and crushing, nature of poverty, for one thing, calls in question our too easy acceptance of our relative affluence and comfortable standard of living – and cries out to us to be profoundly and continually disturbed until poverty is removed from our society. All efforts at confronting and removing poverty must be examined, and where possible supported by Christians, no matter how threatening such efforts may be to ourselves, and even if they are, as they mostly have been, from 'the top down' rather than 'from the bottom up'.

Poverty is an offence to God precisely because it breaks and crushes human beings made in his image; and in our society today, poverty is breaking and crushing us all, not only the poor, for it is our humanity, as well as that of the poor, that is lessened and distorted as we allow poverty to exist in our midst.

John Harvey

Heaven shall not wait

Heaven shall not wait,
for the poor to lose their patience,
the scorned to smile, the despised to find a friend:
Jesus is Lord;
he has championed the unwanted;
in him injustice confronts its timely end.

Heaven shall not wait
for the rich to share their fortunes,
the proud to fall, the elite to tend the least;
Jesus is Lord;
he has shown the master's privilege –
to kneel and wash servants' feet before they feast.

Heaven shall not wait
for the dawn of great ideas
thoughts of compassion divorced from cries of pain:
Jesus is Lord;
he has married word and action;
his cross and company make his purpose plain.

Heaven shall not wait
for triumphant Hallelujahs,
when earth has passed and we reach another shore
Jesus is Lord;
in our present imperfection;
his power and love are for now and then for evermore.

John L. Bell and Graham Maule

INTERFAITH

Ventures in faith

A cluster of four villages in Bungsipsee in Chaiyapoon Province in North-East Thailand invited a student team to live with them and work with them for some weeks in the development of their common life. I was invited to join in an enterprise in the early 1970s which attracted students from all the universities of Thailand. It was sponsored by Roman Catholics but Buddhists in the team outnumbered Christians by five to one. Tiny girls who had never handled a mattock or any other agricultural implement in their lives soon learned the swing which puts the work on the iron head rather than on human arms, and grew adept at working in cement and concrete to make water tanks.

It was an exercise in mutual respect and understanding between people of different faiths. In the morning the Thai flag was raised and people gathered together for a short period of Buddhist prayer and meditation. Each evening, after an evaluation session, the Christians were accustomed to hold an act of worship. After some time Buddhist students said, 'Many of us believe in God too; may we join in?' They were made welcome. Soon Buddhists were reading Old and New Testament lessons, singing hymns, offering prayers, as part of a total trusting company.

It was an exercise in human development. The villagers had their lives enlarged while the students learned to respect the wisdom and values of rural people. They went back much more fully developed human beings.

It was an exercise in wholeness. Village sanitation and personal health care, shared manual work, awareness of rural needs, growth in joint action, worship and prayer, Christian/Buddhist understanding, theological reflection – all these strands – were tied into one bundle of life.

Ian M Fraser

Nonviolence and Peacekeeping

Prayer for Hiroshima Day: August 6th

God, today in sorrow we remember and share our grief.

The few seconds of annihilating time
at Hiroshima and Nagasaki that seared itself for ever
into the depth of our present existence.
Those who died, those who wish they had died
and those who live never to forget:
WE REMEMBER

The many thousands all over the world
who sighed with relief at the ending
of six long years of war.
Those who died,
those whose suffering made them long for death,
those whose experiences seared their lives
and hopes for ever,
those who waited, mourned,
and lived lives of regret at home:
WE REMEMBER

The scientists, politicians, engineers, technicians
and members of the armed forces
who came to realise the awesome power and
responsibility of new technology,
and who live with the results of that knowledge:
WE REMEMBER

The present generation,
growing up in a changed world
overshadowed by the threat of extinction,
feeling helpless in the web of events:
WE REMEMBER

We acknowledge our share of the pain and the responsibility.

God, in Christ you showed us
that you are not removed from us
but share in our agony and suffering.
You are the mother holding her child from the blast,
you are the tortured prisoner longing for release,
you are the war-weary soldier,
you are the scientist pacing the midnight hour,
you are the child with nuclear nightmares,
you know and suffer our human condition.

We know that nothing can separate us from your love.
We pray for your love to enfold us in comfort
your love to share our agony
your love to inspire us to love one another
your love to live in hope.

Helen Steven

Month 4 Day 27

BASIC CHRISTIAN COMMUNITIES

With new gifts in his torn hands

Members of a basic Christian community in Bordeaux explained to me some years ago that, in a city where everything was in movement, a small community might just last for about two years and then members would disperse. 'But we disperse as seed – wherever we settle next, communities will sprout.' Contrast this attitude with a determination to secure the Church into the future which can only be done in terms of the present and the past, while Jesus Christ is ready to come from the future with new gifts in his torn hands.

Ian M Fraser

COMMITMENT

After Psalm 19

The sky does it simply, naturally
day by day by day
the sun does it joyfully
like someone in love
like a runner on the starting-line
the sky, the sun,
they just can't help themselves
no loud voices, no grand speeches
but everyone sees, and is happy with them.

Make us like that, Lord
so that our faith is not in our words but in our lives
not in what we say, but in who we are
passing on your love like an infectious laugh:
not worried, not threatening, just shining
like the sun, like a starry night,
like a lamp on a stand,
light for life –
your light for our lives.

Kathy Galloway

THE REDISCOVERY OF SPIRITUALITY

Spiritual giants

Moses is recognised as a person of deep spirituality not simply because he prized the prophetic ecstasy into which God threw fifty leaders and wished that all the people could be prophets.

He is regarded as a spiritual giant because he had to struggle with his past history of being a murderer, with his dubious identity as an Egyptian-sounding Jew, with his stammer.

And he had to struggle with recurrent aggression and antipathy from the very people he had delivered from slavery, a battle which forced him to shout at God regarding his 'charges',

> *Am I their mother?*
> *Have I brought them into this world*
> *and am I called to carry them in my arms*
> *like a nurse with a baby,*
> *to a land promised by you on oath to their fathers?*
> (Numbers 11:12)

David is seen as a person of deep spirituality not just because he won victory after victory for God from adolescence onwards, not just because he was anointed as God's chosen by Samuel, nor even because he had a prodigious talent for words and music.

He is regarded as a spiritual giant because, among other things, he had to cope with the incessant jealousy of his father-in-law. And he had to deal with the guilt of being a murderer and an adulterer, as well as with the grief of losing his firstborn.

And if we move into the New Testament, we will similarly find that the attestation of Paul's fitness to being a person of deep spirituality comes, of course, from his special visitation and calling as an apostle, his religious pedigree and his theological astuteness.

But it is also attributable to how he coped with his thorn in the flesh, a disputatious church at Corinth, and persecution by fellow Jews and Roman officialdom.

No one … no one … no one … who is regarded as a spiritual giant had it easy, did only what they wanted to do, got exactly what they liked.

Amen says Francis of Assisi, the impoverished one;
Amen says John of the Cross, the tormented one;
Amen says Columba of Iona, the exiled one;
Amen says Hildegaard of Bingen, the suspected one;
Amen says Julia of Norwich, the infirm one;
Amen says Martin Luther, the doubting one;
Amen says Teresa of Avila, the discouraged one;
Amen says Helder Camera, the controversial one;
Amen says Dorothee Solee, the disregarded one.

There is no authentic spirituality, there is no deep faith conviction, there is no true devotion which emanates from a life which is constantly pleasure-filled and pain-free. All the true saints of God never got what they wanted, did what they liked, or lived on cloud nine. So when we, in our present cultural context, wish to define or distinguish the role and purpose of spirituality, it is not to legitimise escapism. It is to enable flaccid hedonists to face up to what they would rather avoid.

John L. Bell

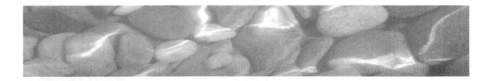

THE THIRTY-FIRST DAY

Elemental

When my time is over
and fire has consumed
all flesh, take my dust
and scatter it
where you can feel
earth, water, rushing air
that I may be
whole.

Then take away with you
memories, burning in fire,
fresh as air, rolling as the sea,
still as the earth
and this shall be
my resurrection.

Joy Mead

End Piece

For a little while, I was the guest of a woman who lived in a poor quarter of San Jose, Costa Rica. She had little education, and her home, like all the houses around, was sub-standard and tiny for the eleven members of her family who lived there. Her husband left at five in the morning each day and worked until seven at night selling vegetables to support the family. They both belonged to a neighbourhood group which tried to see how changes which were needed in the area could be brought about.

One morning the woman was chatting with her friend. She said that the whole community must be roused to press for a fairer deal. Her friend protested that this was rather the responsibility of the local government officials. The tone sharpened: (I was within earshot)

'Do you believe in Jesus Christ?'

'Yes.'

'Do you think Jesus Christ came to change life so that it was more the kind of life God wanted to see, or to leave it as it is?'

'I suppose to change it. Yes, to change it.'

'Do you think Jesus Christ meant to change life by himself, or did he mean us to share the work with him?'

(Hesitantly) 'I know he meant us to play a part.'

'Then how can you believe in Jesus Christ and let things stay as they are?'

Ian M Fraser

Prayers for the Days

Day 1

'New ways to touch the hearts of all'

Pray for 'new ways to touch the hearts of all'.

For writers, musicians, artists, dancers, liturgists …
For all those working creatively in the fields of politics,
community development, human relations …

For risk takers,
for enablers …

God, you are always calling your people
to follow you into the future,
inviting them to new ventures, new challenges,
new ways to care,
new ways to touch the hearts of all.
When they become fearful of the unknown, give them courage.
When they worry that they are not up to the task,
remind them that you would not call them
if you did not believe in them.

When they get tired,
or feel disappointed with the way things are going,
remind them that you can bring change and hope
out of the most difficult situations.

DAY 2

Economic witness

Pray for organisations working to bring about a more just economic order;
people and countries held captive in the chains of debt.

Jesus Christ, Lord of all,
help me to live more simply and
with greater faith in you.

DAY 3

Youth concern

Pray for children
and for youth.

May children be protected and nurtured,
unhindered and encouraged.
May they have the chance to learn,
the space to dance,
the room to grow.

May youth be valued and heard,
supported and challenged,
and be given real opportunities
to help in the reshaping of the church and the world.

Day 4

The Word

For the word of God in scripture,
for the word of God among us,
for the word of God within us,
thanks be to God

Day 5

Hospitality and welcome

Pray for houses of hospitality and welcome,
for Columban houses.

For those who are not welcomed:
refugees and asylum seekers;
all who are homeless.

Jesus, you were once a refugee.
You knew what it was like
to wander the streets and countryside
without any shelter.

Help me to recognise you in the stranger
and in the people I see every day.

Day 6

This is the day

God, your kindness has brought the gift of a new day.
Help me to leave yesterday,
and not to covet tomorrow,
but to accept the uniqueness of today.

Day 7

Iona

You are an island in the sea, O God,
you are a hill on the shore,
you are a star in the darkness,
you are a staff to the weak.
O, my soul's healer,
when I am lost and tired and stumbling
you shield and support me.
God, help me to give light, love and support to others.

Day 8

Life in community

Pray for all those living and working in intentional communities,
giving thanks for their counter-cultural witness.

For volunteers everywhere.

Prayers for the days

May people find meaningful ways to contribute to their communities.
May their gifts and talents be recognised and encouraged.

DAY 9

Women

Pray for women who are discriminated against,
who are marginalised,
who suffer violence and abuse.

For women bearing heavy responsibilities and pressures:

women on the way to the well
women supporting whole families by themselves …

For equal opportunities
and women's issues.

Jesus, women were always close to you,
did not run away –

from pain
from commitment
from grief and emptiness.

May the contributions, wisdom and strength of women
be recognised in wider society.

DAY 10

Prayer

Our Father in heaven,
hallowed be your name,
your kingdom come,
your will be done on earth as in heaven,
give us today our daily bread,
forgive us our sins
as we forgive those who sin against us,
save us in the time of trial
and deliver us from evil,
for the kingdom, the power
and the glory are yours,
now and for ever. Amen.

DAY 11

Justice and peace

O God,
to those who have hunger give bread,
to us who have bread
give hunger for justice.

DAY 12

The integrity of creation

Pray that nations may have the political will
to protect this fragile planet,
and that people everywhere
may think globally and act locally.

Pray for fair trading organisations
as they seek to guard the rights and incomes
of work forces in developing countries.
Pray for the indigenous peoples of the world.

O Christ, there is no plant in the ground
but it is full of your virtue.
There is no form in the strand
but it is full of your blessing.
There is no life in the sea,
there is no creature in the ocean,
there is nothing in the heavens
but proclaims your goodness.
There is no bird on the wing,
there is no star in the sky,
there is nothing beneath the sun
but proclaims your goodness.

Christ, help me to consider the effects of my lifestyle;
to make daily choices prayerfully.

Day 13

Columban Christianity and the Celtic tradition

Alone with none but thee, my God
I journey on my way.
What need I fear when thou art near,
O King of night and day?
More safe am I within thy hand
than if a host did round me stand.

Day 14

Racism

Pray for racial justice,
for those working to overcome racism in our society,
and pressing for changes in nationality law and immigration policy.

Peace between nations,
peace between neighbours,
peace between lovers,
in love of the God of life.

Day 15

Community

Pray for the local community; community development
and community relations.

Prayers for the days

May diversity be valued, barriers crossed,
and ordinary people empowered.
May neighbourhoods be places
where *all* have a part to play.

Day 16

Pilgrimage

Pray for all pilgrims and seekers
and companions on the way;
for all travellers.

Christ, may I walk together with you,
in solidarity with the poor and
with all of God's creation.

Day 17

Sexuality

Pray for lesbian, gay and transgender rights.

May the One
who has lovingly created human life with such diversity and potential,
be with all who challenge prejudice and abuse of power
and all who work for a fairer, more inclusive society.

Prayers for the days

DAY 18

Healing

Pray for health, wholeness and the ministry of healing.

Compassionate God, use ordinary people,
people with their own needs,
to bring life and hope to others.

DAY 19

Social action

Pray for prisoners of conscience;
for political prisoners;
for those who are tortured
and detained without trial.

Let me not shrink from the social and political demands
of the gospel, O God.
By word and action, education and prayer,
make me an instrument of your peace.

DAY 20

Church renewal

Pray for local church renewal;
our local church community.

Prayers for the days

May your churches be centres of justice and joy, O Christ
where your love is shared,
and your life made real in the world.

DAY 21

Worship

Pray that the worship of the Church may be renewed
through scripture, song and honest prayer.

May worship serve to strengthen and inspire your people
to do what you require, O Lord.

DAY 22

Work

Pray for the unemployed,
for industrial mission,
for those whose work is exploited.

For those who have no work, and those who have too much;
for work that is meaningful and shared;
for a society where people are valued for themselves.

In the name of the God of work and rest.

Prayers for the days

Day 23

Called to be one

Pray for relations between denominations in Britain
and the world.

May differences be celebrated.

May Christians be made one in Jesus,
who died to bring peace and reconciliation.

Day 24

Mission

Pray for church centres
and church organisations;

For an approach which is open, inclusive
and sensitive;

Imaginative and
risk-taking

O God, who gave to your servant Columba
the gifts of courage, faith and cheerfulness,
to carry the word of your gospel to every creature,
grant your church a like spirit and energy.

Day 25

The poor and disadvantaged

Pray for the poor and disadvantaged;

for those who choose to live and work
in areas of multiple deprivation;
for all involved in homeless projects and credit unions.

May the poor become empowered
and the world be turned upside down.

Day 26

Interfaith

Pray for interfaith dialogue;
for people of other faiths and ideologies;
for situations and places in the world
where there is war and conflict.

May people of different faiths and beliefs find understanding
in their common search for meaning.

Nonviolence and peacemaking

Pray for organisations involved in international aid and peace-making;
for individuals working in the peace movement
and engaged in nonviolent resistance;

For victims of war and violence,
for the abolition of nuclear weapons.

Lord, make me instrument of your peace.
Where there is hatred, let me sow love,
where there is injury, pardon
where there is doubt, faith
where there is despair, hope
where there is sadness, joy.
O Divine Master
grant that I may not so much seek
to be consoled as to console,
to be understood as to understand,
to be loved as to love.
For it is in giving that we receive,
it is in pardoning that we are pardoned,
it is in dying that we are born again
to everlasting life.
Amen

Day 28

Basic Christian communities

Pray for basic Christian communities throughout the world,
giving thanks that, amid poverty and oppression,
people are finding a biblical faith that empowers and liberates,
as they work together for grassroots change.

Day 29

Commitment

Christ has no other hands but your hands
to do his work today;
no other lips but your lips
to proclaim the good news;
no other love but your love
to give to the rejected, the lonely,
the persecuted, the marginalised.

Day 30

The rediscovery of spirituality

Pray for the growth and deepening of the spiritual life.

God help me to maintain a spirituality that is both tough and tender,
and to seek you not only in the sacred places
but in the midst and the margins of daily life.

Prayers for the days

Day 31

The thirty-first day

Pray for those who have died
and for those who grieve.

As you were before us at our life's beginning
be you so again at our journey's end.
As you were beside us at our soul's shaping,
God be also at our journey's close.

Prayer for Day 1, Kathy Galloway, *The pattern of our days* (adapted);
Youth prayer for Day 3, Brian Woodcock;
Prayer for Day 4, *Iona Abbey worship book*;
Prayer for Day 6, *Iona Abbey worship book*, traditional (adapted);
Prayer for Day 7 Gaelic traditional/Philip Newell, *Each day & Each night* (adapted);
Prayer for Day 11 is from South America;
Prayer for Day 12, Brian Woodcock/Celtic traditional/Neil Paynter;
Prayer for Day 13 is attributed to St Columba;
Prayer for Day 14, traditional;
Prayer for Day 15, Brian Woodcock;
Prayer for Day 17, Brian Woodcock;
Prayer for Day 18, Brian Woodcock (adapted);
Prayer for Day 19, Brian Woodcock;
Prayer for Day 20, Brian Woodcock;
Prayer for Day 22, Brian Woodcock;
Prayer for Day 24, Prayer for the Iona Community (adapted);
Prayer for Day 27, St Francis of Assisi;
Prayer for Day 28, Brian Woodcock;
Prayer for Day 29, attributed to St Teresa of Avila (adapted)
Prayer for Day 30, Brian Woodcock;
Prayer for Day 31, *Iona Community worship book*, 1988 edition.
Prayer concerns for the days, Brian Woodcock or Neil Paynter;
Other prayers for the days, Neil Paynter

Prayers for the days

BIBLE READINGS

Economic witness
Leviticus 25:10–14; Jeremiah 6:13–16; Matthew 6:19–24; Luke 12:13–27; Luke 12:32–34; Luke 21:1–4

Youth
Matthew 9:18–26; Matthew 11:25–26; Matthew 18:1–6; Matthew 19:13–14; Luke 2:41–52; Luke 7:11–15; Luke 10:21–24; Luke 18:15–17; 1 Timothy 4:11–16

Hospitality and welcome
Genesis 18:1–15; Exodus 22:21; Leviticus 19:33–34; Deuteronomy 24:17; 1 Kings 17:8–24; Matthew 2:13–15; Matthew 10:40–42; Matthew 26:6–13; Luke 10:38–42; Luke 15:11–32; Luke 19:1–10; John 2:1–11; Acts 28:1–10; Hebrews 13:1–2

Women
Genesis 18:11–15; Exodus 2:1–10; Joshua 2:1–7; 1 Samuel 2:1–11; Matthew 26:1–13; Matthew 27:55–56; Matthew 28:1–20; Luke 1:26–45; Luke 1:46–55; Luke 8:1–3; Luke 24:1–12; John 4:27–30; John 19:25–27; Acts 9:36–43; Acts 16:13–15; Acts 18:24–28; Romans 16:1–2; Philippians 4:1–3

Prayer
1 Chronicles 29:10–20; Psalms 4:1–3; 19:14; 39:12; 46:10; 55:1–2; 61; 62:1–2; 66:20; 69:13–18; 84:8–9; 86:1–7; 88; Isaiah 37:14–20; Matthew 6:5–24; Matthew 7:7–13; Matthew 26:38–46; Luke 18:1–14; John 17:1–26; Acts 1:12–14; Acts 4:23–31; Acts 16:25–26; Romans 8:26–27; Ephesians 3:14–21; Philippians 4:4–7; James 5:13–20

Justice and Peace
Old Testament: Genesis 9:8–17; Deuteronomy 30:9–14; 1 Samuel 2:1–10; Psalms 9; 10; 22; 51; 72; 85:10; 96; 97; 98; 113; 140; Proverbs 8:20; Isaiah 2:1–5; 42:1–4; 58:1–12; 61:1–4; 63:15–17; Jeremiah 31:31–34; Amos 5:10–24; Micah 4:1–4; 6:1–8; Malachi 3:1–5

New Testament: Matthew 5:1–20; 16:24–26; 23:1–4, 23–24, 37; 28:1–10; Luke 1:46–55; 4:16–30; 6:20–36; 12:13–21, 32–34; 18:18–29; John 20:19–29; Acts 4:32–36; 2 Corinthians 8:1–9; Ephesians 2:13–22; James 2:1–5; 5:1–6; 1 Peter 3:8–17

The Integrity of Creation

Genesis 1:26–31; Genesis 6–9; Exodus 17:1–6; Job 12:7–10; Job:38; 39; Isaiah 24:4–6; Psalms 8; 29; 46; 65:5–13; 67; 72; 80; 84; 96; 104; 147; 148; Ezekiel 34:18–19; Matthew 6:25–31; John 4:7–14; Romans 8:18–25; Colossians 1:15–20

Racism

Genesis 11:1–9; Luke 10:29–37; Acts 2:1–13; Acts 10:34; Acts 17:22–34; Romans 2:11; Colossians 3:9–15

Community

Psalm 133; Matthew 5:43–48; Matthew 7:1–5; Luke 19:35–40; Luke 22:7–38; John 13:6–20; Acts 2:1–21; Romans 12:9–21; 1 Corinthians 11:17–34; 1 Corinthians 12:1–31; 1 Corinthians 13:1–13; Galatians 5:22–26; Ephesians 4:1–16; Ephesians 4:25–32; Colossians 3:12–17; 1 Thessalonians 4:9–12; 1 Thessalonians 5:11–28; 1 Timothy 6:11–16; Hebrews 12:1–29; James 4:11–12; 1 Peter 3:8–12; 1 John:3:18; 1 John 4:7–12

Pilgrimage

Genesis 12:1; Exodus 15:22–27; Exodus 16:1–36; Numbers 20:2–13; Numbers 21:4–5; 1 Chronicles 29:15; Psalm 23; Jeremiah 31:21; Luke 24:13–29; Ephesians 5:8–10; Hebrews 12:1–2

Relationships

Genesis 2: 15–25; Ruth 1–4; 1 Samuel 18:1–5; Song of Solomon 1–8; John 15:1–17

Healing

Psalms 6; 13; 16; 27:13–14; 28:6–9; 30; 34; 36:7–9; 40:1–3; 42; 51:15–17; 139:1–18; Isaiah 43:1–4; Matthew 5:1–12; Matthew 8:1–17; Matthew 8:28–34; Mark 1:29–45; Mark 5:1–20; Mark 8:22–26; Luke 5:12–26; Luke 13:10–17; John 5:1–18; John 10:10; John 11:1–44; Acts 3:1–10; Acts 8:14–25

Action

Exodus 4:10–16; Matthew 7:21–23; Matthew 11:2–6; Matthew 21:28–32; Matthew 25:34–36, 40; Luke 4:16–21; Luke 11:37–54; Luke 12:32–35; Luke 19:1–10; John 4:1–15; Ephesians 6:13–16; James 1:22–25; James 2:14–26

The Church

Acts 9:31; Acts 11:19–26; 1 Corinthians 1:10–31; Revelation 2:1–22

Worship

Exodus 32:1–6; Psalms 95:1–7; 98:1–6; 100; 134; 149; 150; Amos 5:21–24; Acts

13:13–52; Acts 14:1–7; Acts 18:12–14; 1 Corinthians 14:26

Work
Psalms 118:22; 127:1; 135:15–18; Amos 8:4–6; Matthew 4:18–22; Matthew 11:28–30; Matthew 20:1–16; Matthew 25:37–40; Luke 16:1–18; John 2:13–16; John 6:27–34; Ephesians 2:19–22; 1 Thessalonians 5:12–22; 2 Timothy 2:15; Philemon 23–25; James 5:1–6

Called to be one
John 17:18–23; Acts 2:1–21; Acts 17:22–34; 1 Corinthians 12:12–16, 26–27; Galatians 3:28–29; Ephesians 4:1–16; Colossians 3:1–17

Mission
Psalm 37:31; Matthew 5:13–16; Matthew 10:5–42; Luke 5:1–11; Luke 10:1–20; Luke 21:5–19; Luke 24:44–49; Acts 27:13–26; 2 Corinthians 3:1–3; 2 Corinthians 5:20–21; 2 Corinthians 6:1–13; 2 Corinthians 11:16–33; 2 Timothy 2:1–7

The poor and disadvantaged
Job 24:1–8; Psalms 9:18; 113:2–8; Isaiah 58:6–9; Jeremiah 22:13–16; Matthew 19:16–30; Matthew 25:37–40; Luke 2:1–7; Luke 14:15–24; Luke 16:19–31; Luke 21:1–4; James 2:1–7

Nonviolence and peacekeeping
Isaiah 2:1–4; Isaiah 53:4–7; Matthew 5:9; Matthew 5:38–45; John 18:3–12; Romans 12:14–21; Philippians 4:4–7; Revelation 22:1–2

Commitment
Matthew 3:13–17; Matthew 4:18–22; Matthew 10:5–42; Matthew 14:28–30; Matthew 16:21–28; Matthew 19:16–30; Mark 2:13–17; Mark 10:46–52; Luke 9:57–62; John 15:1–27; Hebrews 13:12–16

The thirty-first day
Psalm 23; Matthew 5:4; Matthew 28:5–6; John 14; 2 Corinthians 4:16–18; Hebrews 12:1–2; Revelation 21:1–4

QUOTATIONS FROM
THE IONA COMMUNITY

During the time I worked in the Community's shop on Iona, there was a pin-board up in the book section where visitors and staff were invited to tack up their favourite quotes, or book suggestions.

Here is a random collection of quotes from the Iona Community, one or two of which readers might like to carry into their day and to share with others.

Personally consumed of the here and now,
we must discover God as here and now.
George MacLeod

People come to Iona looking for peace and quiet,
and go away seeking peace and justice.
Volunteer with the Iona Community

Follow the light you have
and pray for more light
George MacLeod

We must often be bitterly ashamed with ourselves for our petty status-seeking and comfort-loving and fairly blameless and largely useless private lives.
Ralph Morton (*God's frozen people*)

It is Christianity that gave the idea of the individual worth to every soul: it is Christianity also that announced that the individual soul could not be complete except in relation.
John Harvey

Pilgrimage is feet-on-the-ground spirituality.
Jan Sutch Pickard

Why are the prisons not full of Christians breaching the peace?
Roger Gray (*Roger: an extraordinary peace campaigner*)

Prayer is the powerhouse.
Roger Gray

To work is to pray.
Source unknown

Nothing is more urgent for the Church than it should read the signs of the times and know the conditions under which it is living.
Ralph Morton (*The household of faith*)

Worship is the backbone of an embodied and integrated spirituality.
Kathy Galloway

If we believe that God loves each and every one the world over we should be celebrating our diversity, valuing each other's contributions, bringing whole lives into worship of the one who offers us life in all its fullness.
Liz Gibson

Follow truth wherever you find it.
Even if it takes you outside your preconceived ideas of God or life.
Even if it takes you outside your own country
into the most insignificant alien places
like Bethlehem.
Be courageous. But concentrate on your search.
Truth is one. All roads lead to home.
George MacLeod

Let thy Resurrection light radiate all our worship.
George MacLeod (*The whole earth shall cry glory*)

Christian beliefs and values do not stem from social utopian thinking … they are practical. Faith, hope and charity are their working tools in situations where many feel that a rich society, living on tax cuts, have negated the moral responsibilities that would alleviate the growing deprivation of the poor.
Larry Nugent

Living in concrete cities I learned to recognise signs of divine presence in the faces of those with whom I laughed and fought and cried, and to rejoice in dandelions that crept through tarmac wastelands and blossomed into golden stars.
Ruth Burgess

Anyone involved in nonviolence is engaged in changing the unjust structures of society, and surely that is revolution. As Christians we are living the Kingdom now; we are already turning the world upside down.
Helen Steven

The ministry of women has also been a living, dynamic and fundamental reality throughout the history of the Christian church. Women were among the travelling band who followed, listened to and shared with Jesus in his itinerant ministry. Women, including Dorcas, Lydia and Priscilla, helped build up and lead the first generations of Christians. Women developed distinctive ministries – as deacons, deaconesses, widows – in the early undivided church.
Lesley Orr Macdonald (*In good company: women in the ministry*)

For me all healing is amazing, miraculous if you like. The process by which our bodies and minds can be repaired fills me with awe. The complexity of the process of repair of even a small cut, a minor upset, seems to me so much more wonderful because it happens from within. The potential for wholeness and fullness of life is present within individual cells of our bodies.
Margaret Stewart

Somewhere along the line, the word 'No' has to be uttered in the name of a greater 'Yes'. We are called to be peace-makers, and that is a tough business. It is certainly not about being peace-lovers (isn't everybody?) or about being passive-ists. The biblical word for peace – shalom – is a rich concept, involving right relationships with God and human beings. It is a tough, disciplined notion, not to be dispersed in the sentimental twanging of guitars. It is peace-with-justice, and it is cross-shaped …

To say 'No' in today's world in the name of a greater 'Yes' is hard to do alone. It requires communities of resistance, with prayer at their heart.
Ron Ferguson (*Chasing the wild goose*)

God's spirit permeates 'every blessed thing'.
George MacLeod

There is no end of places appropriate for doing theology – political meetings, resistance struggles, law courts, pubs …
(On being asked by some frequenters of the Gargunnock Inn about the details of his case against the Poll Tax, Ian Fraser responded, 'I'll tell you what. I'll put a copy of my case against the Poll Tax on the pub counter and you can read it and judge for yourself.')
Ian M Fraser (*Strange fire*)

The impairment of Christian communion … For some, it will be impaired as long as their churches are silent in the face of violence, exploitation and abuse of women and children. For some, it will be impaired by their church's over-close identification with national or ethnic interest. For some, it will be impaired as long as their churches still hold shares in companies which make armaments. For some, it will be impaired by the fact that their churches still hold shares at all, that they continue to profit from an economic system that inflicts huge preventable poverty on millions of the world's most vulnerable people.

Kathy Galloway

Don't ask why 'God doesn't speak'. Don't stand amazed at his apparent deafness. Don't half listen for his voice somewhere beyond the storm. IT IS THE STORM THAT IS HIS VOICE …
George MacLeod (Sermon broadcast from Iona Abbey)

Light a candle, don't just curse the darkness.
Stanley Hope

If you think this is a coincidence, I wish you a very boring life.
George MacLeod

The resurrection from the dead is no more miraculous than the birth of a child. Walking on water is no more miraculous than walking on earth.
Roger Gray (*Roger: an extraordinary peace campaigner*)

The arms race and the war industry is not divided East/West, not even North/South … It is in fact an assault on the poor.
Helen Steven

I realised with shattering intensity that the Risen Christ is now, right in the centre of life … I saw the stark facts that it is not a question of putting Christ back into politics, but recognising the fact that he is already there.
Roger Gray (*Roger: an extraordinary peace campaigner*)

The one supreme conviction that I cannot get away from and – without any dramatics – am quite willing to die for is that only the spiritual can mould any future worth having for the world.
George MacLeod

May God write a message upon your heart,
bless and direct you,
then send you out
living letters of the Word.
(*Iona Abbey worship book*)

SOME RECOMMENDED BOOKS AND MUSIC
(by Iona Community Members and Associates)

Come all you people: forty shorter songs for worship (music book), John L. Bell ISBN 0947988688 (Wild Goose Publications)

He was in the world: meditations for public worship, John L. Bell ISBN 094798870X (Wild Goose Publications)

States of bliss and yearning: the marks and means of authentic Christian spirituality, John L. Bell ISBN 1901557073 (Wild Goose Publications)

Enemy of apathy: Wild Goose songs vol. 2 (music book), John L. Bell/Graham Maule ISBN 0947988270 (Wild Goose Publications)

Heaven shall not wait: Wild Goose songs vol. 1 (music book), John L. Bell/Graham Maule ISBN 0947988238 (Wild Goose Publications)

Love from below: Wild Goose songs vol. 3 (music book), John L. Bell/Graham Maule ISBN 0947988343 (Wild Goose Publications)

Sent by the Lord: World Church songs vol. 2 (music book), John L. Bell (ed./arr.) ISBN 0947988440 (Wild Goose Publications)

When grief is raw: songs for times of sorrow and bereavement (music book), John L. Bell/Graham Maule ISBN 0947988912 (Wild Goose Publications)

Jesus and Peter: off-the-record conversations, John L. Bell & Graham Maule ISBN 1901557170 (Wild Goose Publications)

Love and anger: songs of lively faith and social justice (music book), John Bell & Graham Maule ISBN 094798898X (Wild Goose Publications)

The Celtic way, Ian Bradley ISBN 0232520011 (Darton, Longman & Todd)

Celtic Christianity: making myths and chasing dreams, Ian Bradley ISBN 0748610472 (Edinburgh University Press)

The colonies of heaven, Ian Bradley, ISBN 0232523371 (Darton, Longman & Todd)

Columba: pilgrim and penitent, Ian Bradley ISBN 0947988815 (Wild Goose Publications)

A book of blessings ... and how to write your own, Ruth Burgess ISBN 1901557480 (Wild Goose Publications)

Praying for the dawn: a resource book for the ministry of healing, Ruth Burgess & Kathy Galloway (eds) ISBN 190155726X (Wild Goose Publications)

Chasing the wild goose: the story of the Iona Community, Ron Ferguson ISBN 1901557006 (Wild Goose Publications)

George MacLeod: a biography, Ron Ferguson ISBN 1901557537 (Wild Goose Publications)

Love your crooked neighbour, Ron Ferguson ISBN 0715207660 (St Andrew Press)

Daily readings with George MacLeod, Ron Ferguson; ed ISBN 1901557448 (Wild Goose Publications)

Salted with fire, Ian M Fraser ISBN 0715207628 (St Andrew Press)

Caring for planet earth: stories and prayers for children, Ian M Fraser ISBN 0715207733 (St Andrew Press)

Walking in darkness and light, Kathy Galloway ISBN 0715207695 (St Andrew Press)

A story to live by, Kathy Galloway ISBN 028105164X (SPCK)

Talking to the bones, Kathy Galloway ISBN 0281049270 (SPCK)

Getting personal, Kathy Galloway ISBN 0281048479 (SPCK)

Struggles to love, Kathy Galloway ISBN 0281047405 (SPCK)

Pattern of our days: liturgies and resources for worship, Kathy Galloway; ed ISBN 0947988769 (Wild Goose Publications)

The whole earth shall cry glory: Iona prayers, George MacLeod ISBN 0947988017 (Wild Goose Publications)

Iona: pilgrim guide, Peter Millar ISBN 185311166X (Canterbury Press)

An Iona prayer book, Peter Millar ISBN 1853112054 (Canterbury Press)

Waymarks: signposts to discovering God's presence in the world, ISBN 1853113360 Peter Millar (SCM/Canterbury Press)

Listening for the heartbeat of God, J. Philip Newell ISBN 028105049X (SPCK)

The book of creation, J. Philip Newell ISBN 1853112410 (SCM/Canterbury Press)

Advent readings from Iona, Jan Sutch Pickard/Brian Woodcock ISBN 1901557332 (Wild Goose Publications)

Dandelions and thistles: biblical meditations from the Iona Community, Jan Sutch Pickard (ed.) ISBN 1901557146 (Wild Goose Publications)

Meditations from the Iona Community, Ian Reid ISBN 1901557022 (Wild Goose Publications)

Iona Abbey worship book ISBN 1901557502 (Wild Goose Publications)

Iona – God's energy, Norman Shanks ISBN 0340721723 (Hodder&Stoughton)

A wee worship book: 4th incarnation, Wild Goose Worship Group ISBN 1901557197 (Wild Goose Publications)

Cloth for the cradle: worship resources for Advent, Christmas and Epiphany, Wild Goose Worship Group ISBN 0947988629 (Wild Goose Publications)

Come all you people (cassette), Wild Goose Worship Group ISBN 0947988696 (Wild Goose Publications)

Come all you people (CD), Wild Goose Worship Group ISBN 1901557405 (Wild Goose Publications)

Heaven shall not wait (cassette), Wild Goose Worship Group ISBN 0947988661 (Wild Goose Publications)

Heaven shall not wait (CD), Wild Goose Worship Group ISBN 1901557456 (Wild Goose Publications)

Love from below (cassette), Wild Goose Worship Group ISBN 0947988637 (Wild Goose Publications)

Love from below (CD), Wild Goose Worship Group ISBN 1901557464 (Wild Goose Publications)

One is the body: songs of unity and diversity (music book), Wild Goose Worship Group ISBN 1901557359 (Wild Goose Publications)

One is the body: songs of unity and diversity (cassette), Wild Goose Worship Group ISBN 1901557367 (Wild Goose Publications)

One is the body: songs of unity and diversity (CD), Wild Goose Worship Group ISBN 1901557375 (Wild Goose Publications)

Sent by the lord (cassette), Wild Goose Worship Group ISBN 0947988653 (Wild Goose Publications)

Sent by the lord (CD), Wild Goose Worship Group ISBN 190155743X (Wild Goose Publications)

Stages on the way: worship resources for Lent, Holy Week and Easter, Wild Goose Worship Group ISBN 1901557111 (Wild Goose Publications)

Many, though not all, of the books quoted from in *This is the Day* are available from Wild Goose Publications. For a catalogue of Wild Goose Publications' books and other products please contact: Wild Goose Publications, Fourth Floor, Savoy House, 140 Sauchiehall Street, Glasgow G23DH

web: www.ionabooks.com

Sources and Notes

Month 1

Day 1

With imagination and a sense of adventure, © Norman Shanks (Profit or Prophecy? Reading the Signs of our Times, *Coracle*, Issue No. 3/5, Life Together).

Day 2

Something must be done about the money boys, by George MacLeod (from 'Cursing the "money boys": an act of witness for economic justice', © Ron Ferguson, in *The pattern of our days*, ed. Kathy Galloway, Wild Goose Publications, 1996).

May it not be long (prayer), by John L. Bell (from *A jubilee liturgy*, Wild Goose Resource Group, 2000) © 2000 WGRG, Iona Community, Glasgow G2 3DH, Scotland.

Day 3

Timothy and Paul, © Jan Sutch Pickard (Youth Week, Iona, 2001).

Day 4

What's special about the Bible, © Ian M Fraser (from *Signs of fire: stories of hope, struggle and faith*, cassette tape, Wild Goose Publications, 1998).

Day 5

'The guests were starting to arrive …', © Brian Woodcock (from *Advent readings from Iona*, ed. Brian Woodcock & Jan Sutch Pickard, Wild Goose Publications, 2000).

Day 6

'The reawakening to mystery …', © Peter Millar (from *A reawakening to mystery*, sermon, Iona Abbey).

'This is the day God has made' (from *The Iona Abbey worship book*, Wild Goose Publications, 2001).

Day 7

Why Iona?, © The Iona Community (from *What is the Iona Community?*, Wild Goose Publications, 2001).

Iona dance, © Alix Brown (*Coracle*, October 1999 - Issue 3/47, The Love That Breaks Open Stone).

Day 8

Volunteers, Life in community, Iona 1938 (from *Drinking from our own wells,* writings from the early Iona Community, Iona Community Archives/ Coracle, Issue No. 3/10, © The Iona Community)

Volunteers, Life in community, Iona 2000, © Neil Paynter (from *Iona moments: a diary*)
Top of Dun I, © Jenni Sophia Fuchs

Day 9

God and man and woman (script), from *Wild Goose Prints no. 2* (Wild Goose Publications, 1988). Words & music by John L. Bell & Graham Maule, © 1988 WGRG, Iona Community, Glasgow G2 3DH, Scotland

Day 10

Give us this day our daily bread, © Kathy Galloway (from 'Transfigured by ceremony', *Coracle*, Issue No.3/6, Common Task/Story/Life)

Grace, © Daniel Rounds, Samantha Jones and Greg Jones (from *The One Loaf*, Joy Mead, Wild Goose Publications, 2001)

Day 11

Not an optional extra, © Peter Millar (from *An Iona Prayer Book*, The Canterbury Press, 1998, Norwich).

Sources Month 1

Day 12

A new awareness is required, © Ron Ferguson (from *Chasing the wild goose: the story of the Iona Community*, Wild Goose Publications, 1998).

'Invisible we see you …', by George MacLeod (from the prayer 'Man is made to rise', *The whole earth shall cry glory*, © The Iona Community, 1985)

Day 13

A balanced rhythm, © Ian Bradley (from *Columba: Pilgrim and Penitent*, Wild Goose Publications, 1996).
Note: 1. Thomas Clancy and Gilbert Márkus, Iona: the earliest poetry of a Celtic monastery (Edinburgh University Press, Edinburgh, 1995) p.113.

Day 14

The lure of the monoculture, extract from 'Against the monoculture' in *States of bliss and yearning* (Wild Goose Publications, 1998) by John L. Bell, © 1998 WGRG, Iona Community, Glasgow G2 3DH, Scotland.

Prayer (This prayer evolved out of a Litany of celebration written for a justice and peace service on the issue of racial justice, which took place in Iona Abbey. Different staff members of the Iona Community were invited to contribute their ideas and details – Dorothy Millar, Neil Paynter, Jan Sutch Pickard, Helen Lambie, Jane Bentley.)

Day 15

God sets us in community, © T. Ralph Morton (*The household of faith*, Iona Community, 1951)

Day 16

'Pilgrimage is …' and Prayers before setting out on a pilgrimage, © Ruth Burgess (from 'Pilgrim liturgy for healing', *Praying for the dawn: a resource book for the ministry of healing*, Wild Goose Publications, 2000).

Day 17

'It's in the arms of my lover ...' © Anna Briggs (from 'Wild uncharted seas', *Dreaming of Eden: reflections on Christianity and sexuality*, ed. Kathy Galloway, Wild Goose Publications, 1997).

Divided people, © Kathy Galloway (from 'The happy fault: beyond innocence', *Dreaming of Eden: reflections on Christianity and sexuality*, ed. Kathy Galloway, Wild Goose Publications, 1997).

Day 18

The undeniable need for absolution, © Kathy Galloway (from 'Transfigured by ceremony', *Coracle* - Issue No. 3/6, Common Task/Story/Life)

A touching place, from *Love from below* (Wild Goose Publications, 1989). Words & arrangement by John L. Bell & Graham Maule, © 1989 WGRG, Iona Community, Glasgow G2 3DH, Scotland. Melody: 'Dream Angus', Scots trad.

Day 19

'The seventh war from now' © Roger Gray (from *Roger: an extraordinary peace campaigner*, Helen Steven, WGP, 1990)

The system, © Maire-Colette Wilkie (from *Protest for peace*, Bernadette Meaden, Wild Goose Publications, 1999)

Day 20

A counter-cultural vision and an eagerness to celebrate, © Norman Shanks (from *Iona – God's energy*, Hodder & Stoughton, 1999. Reproduced by permission of Hodder & Stoughton Ltd.).

Day 21

The wrong tune, © Maxwell Craig (*For God's sake ... unity: an ecumenical voyage with the Iona Community*, ed. Maxwell Craig, Wild Goose Publications, 1998).

Sources Month 1

Day 22

Genesis 1 & 2: Iona, © Jan Sutch Pickard.

Day 23

In any event,© Roger Gray (from *Roger: an extraordinary peace campaigner*, Helen Steven, Wild Goose Publications, 1990).

Day 24

Doing mission Jesus's way, quote from Martin Johnstone (from *Starting where we are: the story of a neighbourhood centre. Liberation theology in practice*, © Kathy Galloway, 1998)

Day 25

Nothing blurred there either, © Erik Cramb (from *Fallen to mediocrity: called to excellence, an affirmation of the spirit of community in Britain*, Wild Goose Publications, 1991)

Day 26

A God of Justice and Mercy, © Runa Mackay (from *Exile In Israel: a personal journey with the Palestinians*, Wild Goose Publications, 1995). The prayer is an ancient Celtic morning prayer from Carmina Gadelica (Floris Books, Edinburgh, 1992).

Day 27

Testimony – Not possible to sit on the fence, © Roger Gray (from Speech to the General Assembly of The Church of Scotland, Church and Nation Day, 24 May 1984, in *Roger: an extraordinary peace campaigner*, Helen Steven, Wild Goose Publications, 1990).

To be a soldier, from *One is the body* (Wild Goose Publications, 2002). Words & music by John L. Bell & Graham Maule, © 2002 WGRG, Iona Community, Glasgow G2 3DH, Scotland.

Sources Month 1

Day 28

By spontaneous combustion of the spirit, © Ian M Fraser (from *Celebrating saints: Augustine, Columba, Ninian,* Wild Goose Publications, 1997).

Day 29

'Follow me', © Jan Sutch Pickard (*Coracle,* October 1998 - Issue 3/42, The Purpose Of Our Unity)

Day 30

Quotes on spirituality:

'Spirituality is the oil ...' extract from *States of bliss & yearning* (Wild Goose Publications, 1998) by John L. Bell, © 1998 WGRG, Iona Community, Glasgow G2 3DH, Scotland.

'That which ultimately moves you ...' © Kathy Galloway

'The true mark of Christian spirituality...' © George MacLeod

'Being spiritual is not the same as being religious ...' © Brian Woodcock (*Coracle,* Issue No. 3/17)

'The Bible writers never use the word "spirituality" ...' © John Harvey (*Coracle,* Issue 3/10)

'Spirituality describes for me ...' © Jack Orr (*Coracle,* July 1997)

'It is of course ultimately a matter of balance ...' © Norman Shanks (from *Iona – God's energy,* Hodder & Stoughton, 1999. Reproduced by permission of Hodder & Stoughton Ltd.).

Day 31

I never wanted to be born, from *He was in the world* (Wild Goose Publications, 1995) by John L. Bell, © 1995 WGRG, Iona Community, Glasgow G2 3DH, Scotland.

Prayer, 'Be Thou, triune God ... ', by George MacLeod (from 'A Veil Thin as Gossamer', *The whole earth shall cry glory,* © The Iona Community, 1985).

MONTH 2

Day 1

The real experts, © John Harvey (Poverty – A Violation of Human Rights, Coracle, Issue No. 3/12, Assault on the Poor)

Day 2

The body was put in a plastic bag, © Ian M Fraser (from *Strange fire: life stories and prayers*, Wild Goose Publications, 1994).

Day 3

Harvest, © Ruth Burgess (from *At ground level*, Wild Goose Publications, out of print)

The ice-cream van, © Rachel McCann (from the article 'Camas: the encounter and exchange', *Coracle*, Issue 3/50, Encounter and Exchange)

Day 4

Revolution as well as revelation, by Norman Shanks (from *Iona – God's energy*, Hodder & Stoughton, 1999. Reproduced by permission of Hodder & Stoughton Ltd.).

Day 5

The need of the stranger, © Maxwell Craig (*For God's sake ... unity: an ecumenical voyage with the Iona Community*, ed. Maxwell Craig, Wild Goose Publications, 1998).

Day 6

Benediction of a day, © George MacLeod (from *Daily readings with George MacLeod*, ed. Ron Ferguson, Wild Goose Publications, 2001). Originally from Sermon on Prayer, July 1955.

Prayer on a given day, © Jan Sutch Pickard (from *Vice Versa*, Church in the Market Place Publications, Buxton Methodist Church SK17 9PQ, ISBN 1 889147 12 8)

Sources Month 2

Day 7

Engagement rather than escape, © Norman Shanks (from *Chasing the wild goose: the story of the Iona Community*, Wild Goose Publications, 1998).

Day 8

Iona weaving, © Jan Sutch Pickard.

Day 9

Nightmares in the garden, © Lesley Orr Macdonald (from *Dreaming of Eden: reflections on Christianity and sexuality*, ed. Kathy Galloway, Wild Goose Publications, 1997).
1 John Milton, extract from Paradise Lost (1.297)

Woman without a name, © Joy Mead (from *Dreaming of Eden: reflections on Christianity and sexuality*, ed. Kathy Galloway, Wild Goose Publications, 1997).

Day 10

The cat and the monkey, © Lynda Wright (*Coracle*, Issue 3/17, Enemy Of Apathy)

Prayer, © Brian Woodcock (from *The Iona Abbey worship book*, Wild Goose Publications, 2001).

Day 11

But does that mean politics?, © Ron Ferguson (from *Chasing the wild goose: the story of the Iona Community*, Wild Goose Publications, 1998).

Day 12

Dominion, © Ghillean Prance (from *The Earth under threat: a Christian perspective*, Wild Goose Publications, 1996)

Day 13

'Iona is almost certainly …', © Ian Bradley (from *Columba: Pilgrim and Penitent*, Wild

Goose Publications, 1996).

Notes:

1 'Oh the life of the world', © Kathy Galloway, can be found in *The Iona Abbey Worship Book*, p. 192, *Songs of God's People*, no. 87 and *Common Ground*, no. 97.

'Dance and sing' by John L. Bell and Graham Maule, © Wild Goose Resource Group, is in *The Iona Abbey Worship Book*, p.104 and in *Heaven Shall Not Wait*, p.20.

2 'We lay our broken world in sorrow at your feet', © Anna Briggs, is in *Songs of God's People*, no. 113 and *Common Ground*, no. 143.

Song: 'We lay our broken world', © Anna Briggs.

Day 14

What is the challenge to Christians and to the churches?, © Stanley Hope (from *A very British monster: a challenge to UK immigration policy*, Wild Goose Publications, 1997)

Prayer, 'Help us to be an inclusive church …', © Yousouf Gooljary-Wright (from the Justice and Peace service, Community Week, 2000)

Day 15

The WIFOM factor, © Norman Shanks (from 'Profit or Prophecy?', *Coracle*, Issue No. 3/5)

Day 16

The pilgrim path, © Peter Millar (from *An Iona Prayer Book*, The Canterbury Press, 1998, Norwich.)

'At Columba's Bay …', © Peter Millar (from *An Iona Prayer Book*, op. cit.)

Day 17

All the parts of the body, © Kathy Galloway (excerpts from the article 'Part of The Body', *Coracle*, Issue No. 3/42, Oct 1998, The Purpose Of Our Unity)

Dancing on the edge, © Alix Brown (*Coracle*, Issue 3/47, The Love That Breaks Open Stone)

Day 18

All healing is of God, © George MacLeod (from 'Praying for Healing', *Coracle* 1954)

Prayer: Watch now dear Lord (from *The Iona Abbey worship book*, Wild Goose Publications, 2001).

Day 19

Put your money where your mouth is!, © Adrian Rennie (from 'To Shop is to Pray', *Coracle*, Issue No. 3/16).

Day 20

We would rather do it with you, quote from Martin Johnstone (from *Starting where we are: the story of a neighbourhood centre. Liberation theology in practice*, © Kathy Galloway, 1998).

Day 21

Worship renews life, © Ian M Fraser (from *Strange fire: life stories and prayers*, Wild Goose Publications, 1994).

Day 22

Industrial mission, © Ian M Fraser (from *Strange fire: life stories and prayers*, Wild Goose Publications, 1994).

Day 23

All things in Christ, © Norman Shanks (from *Iona – God's energy*, Hodder & Stoughton, 1999. Reproduced by permission of Hodder & Stoughton Ltd.).

Day 24

God's sphere of activity is the world, © Norman Shanks (from *Iona – God's energy*, Hodder & Stoughton, 1999. Reproduced by permission of Hodder & Stoughton Ltd.).

Sources Month 2

Day 25

'The gospel is about good news to the poor', © Helen Steven.

Prayer: 'Lord God, you humble me before the poor', © Ian M Fraser (from *Strange fire: life stories and prayers*, Wild Goose Publications, 1994).

Day 26

Sharing Communion, by George More (from *A way to God: a biography of George More*, Mary More with Ron Ferguson, © The Iona Community, Wild Goose Publications, 1991).

Day 27

Sword into ploughshares, © George MacLeod (from *Sermon in stone: the story of the Iona Community*, video).

God's agenda, © Norman Shanks (from 'An Engaged Spirituality: An Agenda For Change', Address to the General Assembly of the Church of Scotland, 1996, *Coracle*, July 1996).

Day 28

Life shared, © Ian M Fraser (from *Strange fire: life stories and prayers*, Wild Goose Publications, 1994).

Day 29

Going under (script), from *Jesus & Peter* (Wild Goose Publications, 1999) by John L. Bell & Graham Maule, © 1990, 1999 WGRG, Iona Community, Glasgow G2 3DH, Scotland

Day 30

A liberation theology story, © Kathy Galloway (from *Starting where we are: the story of a neighbourhood centre. Liberation theology in practice*).

Day 31

To die healed, © Tom Gordon (from *Praying for the dawn: a resource book for the ministry of healing*, ed. Ruth Burgess and Kathy Galloway, Wild Goose Publications, 2000).

Sources Month 2

Month 3

Day 1

Beauty beyond words, © Eric Wojchik (from 'A Letter to Land and Sky', *The Track*)
1 The Camas Centre, Ardfenaig, Bunessan, Isle of Mull PA67 6DX, UK. For information please contact: The Camas Administrator, Iona Abbey, Isle of Iona, Argyll PA76 6SN, UK.

Day 2

The way in the world, © John Harvey (from 'The Way In The World', *Coracle*, Issue No.3/3, Having Your Cake … Christians and Money).

Prayer: 'Eternal God …', © Brian Woodcock (from *The Iona Abbey worship book*, Wild Goose Publications, 2001).

Day 3

A litany of intercession (adapted), © Kathy Galloway (*Coracle* Issue No. 3/11, Coming To Birth: A Labour Of Love) (Also appears in *Talking to the bones*, SPCK).

Day 4

Which word didn't you understand?, © Roger Gray (from a sermon, 1979, in *Roger: an extraordinary peace campaigner*, Helen Steven, Wild Goose Publications, 1990).

Day 5

Encounter, © Jan Sutch Pickard (*Coracle* 3/50, Encounter and Exchange).

Day 6

His body now, by T. Ralph Morton (*The household of faith*, Iona Community, 1951).

Day 7

Communities of resistance, © Ron Ferguson (from *Chasing the wild goose: the story of the Iona Community*, Wild Goose Publications, 1998).

Sources Month 3

Prayer: 'Thank you for our time in community …', © David Coleman (from *The pattern of our days*, ed. Kathy Galloway, Wild Goose Publications, 1996).

Day 8

Two women, © Frances Hawkey (*Coracle*, Issue 3/54, Living On The Knife-Edge).

Day 9

My dirty womb, © Kathy Galloway (from 'The happy fault: beyond innocence', *Dreaming of Eden: reflections on Christianity and sexuality*, ed. Kathy Galloway, Wild Goose Publications, 1997).

A labour of love, © Kathy Galloway (from Wild Goose Prints no. 3: Sketches & Scripts for Worship & Discussion).

Day 10

Silence, © Giles David, (from *The pattern of our days*, ed. Kathy Galloway, Wild Goose Publications, 1996).

Day 11

An informed anger, by Joy Mead (from *Compassion in the marketplace*, Wild Goose Publications, 1997).

Inspired by love and anger from *Love & anger* (Wild Goose Publications, 1997), words & arrangement by John L. Bell & Graham Maule, © 1987 WGRG, Iona Community, Glasgow G2 3DH, Scotland. Melody: 'Salley gardens', Irish trad.

Day 12

Every time we see a rainbow, © John Harrison, published here for the first time.
1 *Energy – The Changing Climate*, HMSO, RCEP. Can be downloaded from http://www.rcep.org.uk
2 *Contraction and Convergence - The Global Solution to Climate Change*

Day 13

Walking together, © Ian M Fraser (from *Celebrating saints: Augustine, Columba, Ninian*, Wild Goose Publications, 1997).

Day 14

We have a choice, © Stanley Hope (from 'Light a Candle', *Coracle*, Issue 3/17, Enemy Of Apathy).

The monster, © Stanley Hope (*A very British monster: a challenge to UK immigration policy*, Wild Goose Publications, 1997).

Day 15

Can 'community' return, © Peter Millar (from *Waymarks: signposts to discovering God's presence in the world*, The Canterbury Press, 2000, Norwich).

East 53rd Street, Chicago, © Peter Millar (from *Waymarks*, op. cit.)

Day 16

A counter-cultural journey, © Peter Millar (from *A reawakening to mystery*, sermon, Iona Abbey).

The walk of faith, © Kathy Galloway (from an editorial, *Coracle*, Issue No. 3/33)

'Bless to us O God' (from *The Iona Abbey worship book*, Wild Goose Publications, 2001).

Day 17

Why should this be so difficult, © Neil Squires (from 'Sexuality and the Iona Community', *Coracle*, Issue 3/58: Inside Out: sexuality, inclusion and exclusion)

Day 18

Renaming ourselves, extract from 'The renaming of God' in *States of bliss and yearning* (Wild Goose Publications, 1998) by John L. Bell, © 1998 WGRG, Iona Community, Glasgow G2 3DH, Scotland.

Day 19

Give me a drink, extract from 'The lawbreaker and the evangelist' in *States of bliss and yearning* (Wild Goose Publications, 1998) by John L. Bell, © 1998 WGRG, Iona Community, Glasgow G2 3DH, Scotland.

Day 20

Loitering with intent, © Ewan Aitken (from 'Loitering with intent', July 2001, *Life & Work Magazine*).

Day 21

As much an offering to God as anything done in church, © John Harvey.

Day 22

The power of ceremony, © Kathy Galloway (from 'Transfigured By Ceremony', *Coracle*, Issue No.3/6 Common Task/Story/Life).

Christ the worker, by Tom Colvin, an early member of the Iona Community. Copyright © 1969 Agape/Hope Publishing Co. Administered by CopyCare Ltd, PO Box 77, Hailsham, E. Sussex BN27 3EF, UK. (e-mail: music@copycare.com) Used by permission.

Day 23

'Open to all', © Maxwell Craig (*For God's sake ... unity: an ecumenical voyage with the Iona Community*, ed. Maxwell Craig, Wild Goose Publications, 1998).

Day 24

Moratorium on mission, © Ian M Fraser (from *Strange fire: life stories and prayers*, Wild Goose Publications, 1994).

Day 25

The meaning of the Eucharist, © Ian M Fraser (from *Strange fire: life stories and prayers*, Wild Goose Publications, 1994).

Sources Month 3

Among the poor (originally titled 'He is coming') (responses), from *Cloth for the cradle* (Wild Goose Publications, 1997) by John L. Bell, © 1997 WGRG, Iona Community, Glasgow G2 3DH, Scotland

Day 26

Uncle Wes, poem from a letter from Australia/Wellspring Community, © Peter and Dorothy Millar.
The Wellspring Community is an ecumenical Community of lay and ordained men and women, who are seeking new ways of living the Gospel. Established in 1992, the community is inspired by the Iona Community. Wellspring Members and Friends live in all areas of Australia. They have identified the following areas of concern for prayer and action: Spirituality and Worship, Peace and Social Justice, Aboriginal Reconciliation, The Environment, Ecumenical & Interfaith Issues. (Wellspring Community Inc leaflet)

The Wellspring Community, PO Box 488, Mt Druitt NSW 2770, Australia
ph 02 9835 2970; fax 02 9835 2730; e-mail annesmcp@aol.com

Day 27

Some of the most violent people I have met are pacifists, © Helen Steven (from 'Justice and Peace Join Hands: Further Probing with Ian M Fraser', *Coracle*, Feb 2000).
1 Ian M Fraser, from 'Probe: Kosovo and Nonviolence', Coracle Issue 3/49.

An idea whose time has come, © Helen Steven (from 'Non-Violent Soldiers Of Christ', *Coracle*, Issue No. 3/8).

Day 28

A community at worship, © Ian M Fraser (from *Strange fire: life stories and prayers*, Wild Goose Publications, 1994).

Day 29

Will you come and follow me?, from *Heaven shall not wait* (Wild Goose Publications, 1987). Words & arrangement by John L. Bell & Graham Maule, © 1987 WGRG, Iona Community, Glasgow G2 3DH, Scotland. Melody: 'Kelvingrove' Scots trad.

Sources Month 3

Day 30

The incarnation, © Ron Ferguson (from *Chasing the wild goose: the story of the Iona Community*, Wild Goose Publications, 1998).

Lord Jesus, it's good to know, © Kathy Galloway, (from *The pattern of our days*, ed. Kathy Galloway, Wild Goose Publications, 1996).

Day 31

'In the midst of death there is life', © Erik Cramb (from *Parables and patter,* out of print).

Month 4

Day 1

And the peacemakers began to dance, © George Charlton (from 'No More Trident', *Coracle,* June 2000 - Issue 3/50 / The Iona Community Annual Report 2000).

Day 2

Kingdom values, © Erik Cramb (from *Fallen to mediocrity: called to excellence, an affirmation of the spirit of community in Britain,* Wild Goose Publications, 1991).

Day 3

Heavenly bodies, © Iona Millar.
Just a thought, © Katie Hacking.

Day 4

Brainstorming the Bible, © Kathy Galloway (from *Starting where we are: the story of a neighbourhood centre. Liberation theology in practice,* © Kathy Galloway, 1998).

Day 5

Serving in the shop (Isle of Iona), © Neil Paynter.

Day 6

The kingdom is near, © Kathy Galloway (*Coracle*, Issue 3/17, Enemy of Apathy).

Day 7

'A place of hope', © Peter Millar (from *An Iona Prayer Book*, The Canterbury Press, 1998, Norwich).

Day 8

Reflection from Iona, © Neil Paynter (*Coracle*, Issue 3/45)

Blessing: 'May God's goodness be yours' (adapted from the Carmina Gadelica, and appears in *The Iona Abbey worship book*, Wild Goose Publications, 2001).

Day 9

If Christ cannot be seen in women, © Chris Polhill (from 'A journey of discovery', *Coracle*, Issue 3/52, Dangerous Ground).

Wholly God, © Ruth Harvey (from *Pushing the boat out*, ed. Kathy Galloway, Wild Goose Publications, 1995).

Day 10

Everyone can pray, © Roger Gray (from *Roger: an extraordinary peace campaigner*, Helen Steven, Wild Goose Publications, 1990).

Think of the Maker, © Kathy Galloway (from *The Iona Community worship book*, 1988 edition, Wild Goose Publications).

Day 11

Hand in hand, © Jan Sutch Pickard (from *Advent readings from Iona*, ed. Brian Woodcock & Jan Sutch Pickard, Wild Goose Publications, 2000).

Day 12

Song: 'Oh the life of the world', words © Kathy Galloway/music © Ian Galloway (from *The Iona Abbey worship book*, Wild Goose Publications, 2001).

Day 13

In the footsteps of Columba today, © Norman Shanks (from the sermon 'Engagement, not escape', Iona Abbey, Columba Week/*Coracle*, August 1997).

Blessing, by St Columba (from *The Iona Abbey worship book*, Wild Goose Publications, 2001).

Day 14

Dropping the adjectives, © Alix Brown (*Coracle*, Issue 3/4, The Love That Breaks Open Stone).

Day 15

Communities of hope are always breaking open, © Kathy Galloway (from 'Put your hand in my side: communities of hope and unity in worship (*For God's sake ... unity: an ecumenical voyage with the Iona Community*, ed. Maxwell Craig, Wild Goose Publications, 1998).

Day 16

Pilgrims or planners, © Norman Shanks (from *Seeds for the morrow: inspiring thoughts from many sources* collected by Dorothy Millar).

To finish, © Kate McIlhagga, (from *The pattern of our days*, ed. Kathy Galloway, Wild Goose Publications, 1996).

Day 17

Christ from a different starting point, © Kathy Galloway (from 'The happy fault: beyond innocence', *Dreaming of Eden: reflections on Christianity and sexuality*, ed. Kathy Galloway, Wild Goose Publications, 1997).

Sources Month 4

Day 18

Renaming others, extract from 'The renaming of God' in *States of bliss & yearning* (Wild Goose Publications, 1998) by John L. Bell, © 1998 WGRG, Iona Community, Glasgow G2 3DH, Scotland.

Day 19

'All good things in the world come from fools with faith', © Norman Shanks (from *Iona – God's energy*, Hodder & Stoughton, 1999. Reproduced by permission of Hodder & Stoughton Ltd.).

Day 20

My vision of church, © Ruth Harvey, excerpts from the essay 'Inside Out' (from *In good company: women in the ministry*, ed. Lesley Orr Macdonald, Wild Goose Publications, 1999).

What gives me hope, © Lynda Wright (from 'Angry At The Church', *Coracle*, Issue No.3/6, Common Task/Story/Life).

Prayer: 'O Christ, you are within each of us', by George MacLeod, © The Iona Community (from *The Iona Abbey worship book*, Wild Goose Publications, 2001).

Day 21

The religious moment flowers from the practical, © Kathy Galloway, (from *The pattern of our days*, ed. Kathy Galloway, Wild Goose Publications, 1996).

An Adomnán liturgy of celebration, © The Adomnán Affinity Group (Maire-Colette Wilkie) and Norman C. Habel (see note 2).
1 Introduction by Neil Paynter drawn from 'Cain Adomnán' (Adomnán's Law), a seventh-century law for the protection of non-combatants, translated with an introduction by Gilbert Markús, OP.
2 The 'Litany of celebration' is adapted from 'Dreams for celebration', © Norman C. Habel from his book *Interrobang* (Lutterworth Press, 1970).
3 'Cain Adomnán' (Adomnán's Law), a seventh-century law for the protection of non-combatants, translated with an introduction by Gilbert Márkus OP, is available from:

Blackfriars Books, 2 Glenogle House, Stockbridge Colonies, Edinburgh EH3 5HR. Copies £3 each, including postage.

Day 22

The Gospel and the physical (from Iona Community archives).

The rebuilding of lives, © Norman Shanks (from *The Iona Community: today's challenge, tomorrow's hope*, video, WGP, 2001)

Day 23

Think global – act local, © Murdoch MacKenzie (from 'Think global – act local (*For God's sake ... unity: an ecumenical voyage with the Iona Community*, ed. Maxwell Craig, Wild Goose Publications, 1998).

Hope for the world (litany), by John L. Bell, from *Iona Community worship book* (Wild Goose Publications, 1987) © 1987 WGRG, Iona Community, Glasgow G2 3DH, Scotland

Day 24

An enormous need, quotes by Kathy Galloway and Martin Johnstone (from *Starting where we are: the story of a neighbourhood centre. Liberation theology in practice*, © Kathy Galloway, 1998).

Song: 'Sent by the Lord am I', words © Jorge Maldonado, music arr. Wild Goose Resource Group (From *Sent by the Lord: World Church songs Vol. 2*, Wild Goose Publications, 1991).

Day 25

An offence to God, © John Harvey, from his book *Bridging the gap: has the church failed the poor?*, published by Saint Andrew Press, 1987, Edinburgh.

Heaven shall not wait, from *Heaven shall not wait* (Wild Goose Publications, 1987), words & music by John L. Bell & Graham Maule, © 1987 WGRG, Iona Community, Glasgow G2 2DH, Scotland.

Day 26

Ventures in faith, © Ian M Fraser (from *Signs of fire: stories of hope, struggle and faith*, cassette tape, Wild Goose Publications, 1998).

Day 27

Prayer for Hiroshima Day, © Helen Steven, (from *The pattern of our days*, ed. Kathy Galloway, Wild Goose Publications, 1996).

Day 28

With new gifts in his torn hands, © Ian M Fraser (from *Celebrating saints: Augustine, Columba, Ninian*, Wild Goose Publications, 1997).

Day 29

After Psalm 19, © Kathy Galloway, (from *The pattern of our days*, ed. Kathy Galloway, Wild Goose Publications, 1996).

Day 30

Spiritual giants, extract from 'Dubious beatitudes' in *States of bliss and yearning* (Wild Goose Publications, 1998) by John L. Bell, © 1998 WGRG, Iona Community, Glasgow G2 3DH, Scotland.

Day 31

Elemental , © Joy Mead is published here for the first time.

End Piece, © Ian M Fraser (from *Strange fire: life stories and prayers*, Wild Goose Publications, 1994).

The Iona Community

The Iona Community, founded in 1938 by the Revd George MacLeod, then a parish minister in Glasgow, is an ecumenical Christian community committed to seeking new ways of living the Gospel in today's world. Initially working to restore part of the medieval abbey on Iona, the Community today remains committed to 'rebuilding the common life' through working for social and political change, striving for the renewal of the church with an ecumenical emphasis, and exploring new, more inclusive approaches to worship, all based on an integrated understanding of spirituality.

The Community now has over 240 Members, about 1500 Associate Members and around 1500 Friends. The Members – women and men from many denominations and backgrounds (lay and ordained), living throughout Britain with a few overseas – are committed to a fivefold Rule of devotional discipline, sharing and accounting for use of time and money, regular meeting, and action for justice and peace.

At the Community's three residential centres – the Abbey and the MacLeod Centre on Iona, and Camas Adventure Camp on the Ross of Mull – guests are welcomed from March to October and over Christmas. Hospitality is provided for over 110 people, along with a unique opportunity, usually through week-long programmes, to extend horizons and forge relationships through sharing an experience of the common life in worship, work, discussion and relaxation. The Community's shop on Iona, just outside the Abbey grounds, carries an attractive range of books and craft goods.

The Community's administrative headquarters are in Glasgow, which also serves as a base for its work with young people, the Wild Goose Resource Group working in the field of worship, a bi-monthly magazine, *Coracle*, and a publishing house, Wild Goose Publications.

For information on the Iona Community contact:
The Iona Community
Fourth Floor, Savoy House,
140 Sauchiehall Street, Glasgow G2 3DH, UK
Phone: 0141 332 6343
e-mail: ionacomm@gla.iona.org.uk   web: www.iona.org.uk

For enquiries about visiting Iona, please contact:
Iona Abbey
Isle of Iona
Argyll PA76 6SN, UK
Phone: 01681 700404   e-mail: ionacomm@iona.org.uk

For book/tape/CD catalogues, contact:
Wild Goose Publications
Fourth Floor, Savoy House,
140 Sauchiehall Street, Glasgow G2 3DH, UK
e-mail: admin@ionabooks.com
Phone: 0141 332 6292
or see our products online at www.ionabooks.com

'Iona can be the home of the New Reformation. But it must recover its genius: keep acting its insights at whatever risk if its insights are to be clarified and the next obedience seen. If, as a community, we write at all it can be no more than passing calculations in the sand, to point to the next Obedience.'

George MacLeod